Adultbrain Publishing is dedicated to breathing new life into timeless literary works by resurrecting old classics for the modern age. We meticulously curate and convert these masterpieces into high-quality digital and audio formats, making them accessible to a new generation of readers and listeners. Our commitment to preserving the essence of these works, while enhancing them with today's technology, allows us to offer immersive experiences that retain the authenticity of the original texts. Whether rediscovering a beloved classic or experiencing it for the first time, our editions invite readers to start using their Adultbrain today.

Published by Adultbrain Publishing.

ISBN: 978-1-998614-14-1
Title: Legacy of Lies: The Trudeau Dynasty
Start using your Adultbrain today.
For more information, visit: www.adultbrain.ca

Legacy of Lies:
The Trudeau Dynasty

Will Stickle

Introduction

The Rise of a Political Dynasty

The Trudeau family, synonymous with Canadian politics for decades, has cast a long shadow over the nation's governance, first through Pierre Elliott Trudeau and now through his son, Justin Trudeau. Both figures have shaped Canada in ways that few political families could dream of, with policies that continue to polarize the country. The story of their influence is one of charisma, ideological drive, and controversial decisions that have left Canada divided and, some would argue, crippled under the weight of their legacy.

Pierre Elliott Trudeau: The Charismatic Architect of a Centralized Canada

Pierre Trudeau burst onto the Canadian political scene with a flair that was unmatched by any of his contemporaries. Elected as the 15th Prime Minister in 1968, he brought a new wave of progressive liberalism, dressed up in charisma and intellectualism. His "Trudeaumania" was a media phenomenon that had never been seen before in Canadian politics. But behind the glamour, his tenure was marked by policies that centralized power in Ottawa at the expense of provincial autonomy, particularly alienating the Western provinces.

Pierre's ideological leanings leaned heavily toward socialism, disguised as "Just Society" liberalism. His cozy relationships with communist regimes like that of Fidel Castro in Cuba—whom he visited with admiration—showed a man who was more aligned with centralized control and state-driven economics than with free markets. The National Energy Program (NEP), one of his most infamous policies, exemplified this. Ostensibly designed to secure Canada's energy independence, it instead siphoned wealth from resource-rich provinces like Alberta, transferring economic power to the federal government and crippling the West's economy. Pierre's legacy is seen in this continued East vs. West divide, a deep fracture in Canadian unity that persists to this day.

The War Measures Act: A Dictator's Move in a Democratic Country

Pierre's use of the War Measures Act during the October Crisis of 1970 is often cited as one of the darkest moments in modern Canadian history. In response to the FLQ kidnappings in Quebec, Trudeau suspended civil liberties across the country. While some saw this as a necessary measure to combat terrorism, others recognized it as a blatant overreach of power. Trudeau deployed the military onto Canadian streets, rounding up citizens without due process, all under the pretext of national security. In his famous response to critics of this authoritarian maneuver, he quipped, "Just watch me." And watch, Canadians did—as their rights were trampled under the boot of a state that positioned itself above the law.

This was a hallmark of Pierre Trudeau's tenure: using crises to justify government overreach. Whether it was silencing dissent or manipulating the economy, Trudeau Sr.'s legacy is one of placing government control above individual freedoms. His manipulation of media, his iron grip on civil liberties, and his disregard for regional concerns continue to serve as an unsettling template for governance today.

Justin Trudeau: Inheritance of Power Without Competence

Fast-forward to 2015, and the Trudeau name again graced the Prime Minister's office, this time with Pierre's son, Justin Trudeau. If Pierre was the architect of a centralized, quasi-authoritarian Canada, Justin has been the executor, entrenching his family's political legacy through virtue signaling and empty platitudes. Elected on a platform of transparency, reconciliation, and progressivism, Justin's tenure has been anything but. His administration has been riddled with scandal, from the SNC-Lavalin affair, where he was accused of political interference in a criminal case to protect a Quebec-based firm, to the WE Charity scandal, which exposed his family's financial ties to a dubious charitable organization that received a lucrative government contract without due diligence.

But Justin Trudeau's influence goes far beyond these scandals; he has pushed Canada further down a path of divisive identity politics and globalist agendas. Under his leadership, the media has been bought off with taxpayer money, ensuring a constant stream of positive coverage while suppressing dissenting voices. His government has also positioned Canada as a pawn in globalist circles, from his enthusiastic promotion of the UN's migration pact to his cozy relationship with the World Economic Forum. Like his father, Justin's policies have alienated Western Canada, exacerbating the country's already deep regional divides.

A Dynasty of Division and Globalism

Together, the father and son duo have shaped Canada into a state that is increasingly beholden to the federal government, eroding provincial rights, individual freedoms, and the country's sovereignty. Pierre started the process with his heavy-handed economic policies, ideological leanings, and manipulation of crises to expand governmental powers. Justin has simply carried on the family tradition, only now under the guise of progressive values, environmentalism, and reconciliation.

Yet, behind the carefully curated media image, the Trudeau family has been central to Canada's growing problems. From Pierre's socialist-inspired policies to Justin's neoliberal corporatism wrapped in identity politics, the family's influence has only deepened the fractures in Canadian society. The Trudeau name is no longer just synonymous with charisma and charm—it has become a symbol of corruption, government overreach, and a betrayal of Canadian values.

The Trudeau dynasty's influence is not one of national unity or progress but one of division, control, and a systematic erosion of Canadian autonomy. The country remains in a precarious position, and the question looms: how much longer can Canada endure the consequences of the Trudeau legacy?

The Portrayal of Pierre and Justin Trudeau as Charismatic Leaders, Masking the Alleged Corruption Behind the Scenes

For more than half a century, the Trudeau name has been associated with charisma, charm, and political flair in Canada. Pierre Trudeau, the architect of "Trudeaumania," captivated the nation with his sharp intellect and bold personality. Decades later, his son, Justin Trudeau, rose to prominence with a strikingly similar blend of youthful exuberance and media-friendly soundbites. Both father and son have been expertly marketed as progressive champions of Canadian values, using their personas to mask a political reality steeped in corruption, cronyism, and scandal. This dynamic portrayal—charisma on the surface, corruption behind the scenes—has been central to maintaining their grip on power, deflecting criticisms, and manipulating public opinion.

Pierre Trudeau: The Intellectual Charmer with Authoritarian Tendencies

When Pierre Elliott Trudeau first entered the political arena, he did so with an almost cinematic flair. "Trudeaumania" swept through Canada in the late 1960s, fueled by Pierre's good looks, quick wit, and a sense of rebellion that resonated with a younger generation tired of the political establishment. To the public, Pierre was a breath of fresh air—an intellectual and a renegade who could shake up the stodgy world of Canadian politics. His high-profile lifestyle, including a brief marriage to the glamorous Margaret Sinclair and frequent appearances in the media, only added to his allure. He became not just a political leader, but a cultural icon.

But behind this crafted image lay a darker reality. Pierre's policies, especially his economic interventions, were often cloaked in socialist ideology, centralizing power in Ottawa and controlling key industries in ways that stifled provincial autonomy and economic growth. The most infamous example of this was the National Energy Program (NEP), which funneled wealth from resource-rich provinces like Alberta to the federal government and eastern provinces, effectively strangling the West's economy for political gain. This policy created a deep and lasting divide in Canada, one that still festers today. Yet, Pierre's charm allowed him to gloss over such corruption, presenting these moves as "necessary" for national unity and economic security. The media—then as now—was complicit, rarely challenging Trudeau on the far-reaching implications of his actions.

His friendly ties with dictators like Fidel Castro further exposed the duplicity of his public image. While he spoke of democratic values and freedom, Pierre Trudeau cozied up to a totalitarian regime, praising Castro's "achievements" and often ignoring the brutal oppression of the Cuban people. This cognitive dissonance—preaching liberty at home while supporting tyranny abroad—was only possible because of the sheer force of Pierre's charisma. The Canadian public and much of the media remained largely oblivious or indifferent, dazzled by his intellectual bravado and flamboyant public persona.

Justin Trudeau: The Selfie King with Scandals in His Wake

Decades later, Pierre's son, Justin Trudeau, took up the family mantle, but with a twist more fitting to the social media age. While Pierre's charisma came from his intellectualism and rebelliousness, Justin's appeal was rooted in his youthfulness, his good looks, and his carefully crafted image as a champion of diversity, equality, and progressive politics. To an increasingly image-conscious electorate, Justin Trudeau was a modern, enlightened leader who seemed to embody the values of tolerance and change. His charm came not from grand ideas, but from his ability to connect emotionally, particularly with younger voters, through social media platforms like Twitter and Instagram, where his selfies became a symbol of his "in-touch" persona.

But like his father, this carefully constructed image belied the reality of corruption and cronyism that plagued his administration from the start. Justin Trudeau's government has been embroiled in several major scandals, each one more damning than the last. The SNC-Lavalin scandal is perhaps the most notable, in which Trudeau attempted to interfere with the judicial process to prevent a major Quebec-based corporation from facing corruption charges. This blatant act of political interference led to the resignation of his Attorney General, Jody Wilson-Raybould, and a public outcry over the Trudeau government's deep ties to corporate elites. Despite this, Justin's charm and well-managed media appearances allowed him to weather the storm with minimal political damage. His narrative of being a champion of Canadian workers and values continued to hold sway over a large part of the electorate.

Then came the WE Charity scandal, a case that further exposed the Trudeau family's ties to crony capitalism. The Trudeau government awarded a lucrative contract to the WE Charity organization to manage a youth volunteer program, despite clear conflicts of interest—his family had received hundreds of thousands of dollars in payments from the charity for speaking engagements. While this scandal dented his reputation more visibly than SNC-Lavalin, Justin's ability to present himself as a victim of misunderstanding and partisan attacks allowed him to survive yet another potential downfall. His constant refrains of "inclusivity" and "progress" have acted as shields, deflecting the public from the underlying reality of his administration's corruption.

Media Manipulation: Crafting the Trudeau Myth

One of the key tools that both Pierre and Justin Trudeau have used to maintain their charismatic appeal while masking corruption is the Canadian media. Pierre controlled the narrative through an intellectual approach, engaging with the media in ways that reinforced his image as the thinking man's leader. His speeches, often filled with lofty rhetoric, played well with a Canadian press that was already predisposed to his liberal worldview. Few challenged him on his more questionable policies, and those who did were often marginalized as fringe critics.

Justin, in contrast, has taken a more direct approach—buying the media. Under his administration, the Canadian government allocated hundreds of millions of dollars to bail out struggling media companies, ensuring favorable coverage and soft-pedaling of his administration's failures. This financial control over the media has allowed Justin Trudeau to present himself as a progressive leader even as his government acts in ways that directly contradict those values. The media's refusal to critically examine the extent of his corruption has become a significant enabler of his public image. While dissent exists, it is often marginalized or drowned out by the overwhelmingly positive coverage that comes from outlets with direct financial ties to the government.

This has created a system where the Trudeau legacy—both Pierre's intellectualism and Justin's progressivism—can be perpetuated despite clear evidence of corruption and mismanagement. The charisma that once defined Pierre's reign as a man of ideas has now evolved into Justin's era of curated optics, where selfies and soundbites replace substantive policy, and where scandal is brushed aside with carefully managed media appearances.

The Trudeau family's ability to maintain power and influence in Canadian politics is a testament to the effectiveness of charisma as a political tool. Pierre's intellectual charm allowed him to implement divisive and damaging policies under the guise of national unity and social progress. Justin's media-savvy persona has allowed him to rise above scandals that would have destroyed other politicians. Both have relied on the myth of the Trudeau name, carefully crafted by a complicit media and a political class that benefits from their rule.

Behind the veneer of charm lies a long history of corruption, cronyism, and scandal. From Pierre's authoritarian tendencies and socialist policies to Justin's corporate favoritism and media manipulation, the Trudeau family's legacy is not one of progress or unity, but of division and control. The Canadian public has been sold an illusion for over half a century, and only by looking past the charisma can we see the true cost of the Trudeau dynasty's rule.

Two Generations of Trudeau Leadership and the Harm They've Inflicted on Canada

The Trudeau family has dominated Canadian political life for over half a century, shaping the country through two distinct yet eerily similar periods of leadership under Pierre and Justin Trudeau. Both father and son were elevated by charisma and a media-driven cult of personality, and both have used their time in power to push agendas that many argue have left lasting scars on the nation. To understand the depth of this impact, we need to peel back the layers of their public personas and examine how their policies and decisions have undermined Canada's unity, economic health, and global standing.

The Trudeau Dynasty: A Tale of Two Leaders

Pierre Elliott Trudeau, the intellectual and flamboyant figure who led Canada as Prime Minister for nearly 16 years, was hailed as a visionary by some and vilified as a power-hungry authoritarian by others. His leadership saw the implementation of policies that forever altered the country's socio-political landscape, including the 1982 Constitution Act and the Charter of Rights and Freedoms, which centralized federal power and stripped provinces of much of their autonomy. To his supporters, these moves were about creating a more just and unified Canada, but to his detractors, they were a blatant power grab, sowing the seeds of regional division that would plague the country for decades to come.

Fast forward to 2015, and his son, Justin Trudeau, took up the family's political mantle. Armed with his father's name and a carefully curated image of youthful idealism, Justin's rise to power was swift, bolstered by a media that adored him and a public desperate for a fresh face in Ottawa. His initial platform promised transparency, reconciliation, and progressive change. However, like his father before him, Justin's leadership quickly revealed itself to be marked by scandal, economic mismanagement, and a centralization of power that echoed his father's legacy. As we look more closely at their collective leadership, it becomes clear that the damage inflicted by the Trudeaus is systemic, deep-rooted, and far-reaching.

The Shattered Unity: Regional Divides and Federal Overreach

One of the most glaring consequences of both Pierre and Justin's leadership has been the deepening divide between Canada's regions. Pierre Trudeau's National Energy Program (NEP), introduced in 1980, was perhaps the most notorious example of his disregard for the economic well-being of Western Canada. The program, designed to assert federal control over the oil industry and ensure energy security for the entire nation, ended up devastating Alberta's oil-based economy. Westerners saw this policy as a deliberate attempt to siphon their wealth to benefit the rest of Canada, particularly Quebec and Ontario, reinforcing the perception that the federal government had little regard for the needs of the West.

The economic fallout from the NEP was immediate and long-lasting. Albertans, already feeling alienated from Ottawa, became even more entrenched in their discontent, fostering a Western separatist sentiment that remains alive today. The program's failure exposed a Trudeau family tendency toward centralization—a desire to consolidate power in Ottawa, no matter the cost to the provinces. This approach would be a hallmark of both Pierre and Justin's tenures, manifesting in policies that treated Canada not as a federation of distinct provinces with unique needs, but as a singular entity under the thumb of federal control.

Justin Trudeau's leadership has only exacerbated this regional divide. His carbon tax, imposed on provinces without their consent, is seen as another Ottawa-knows-best solution, particularly in energy-rich provinces like Alberta and Saskatchewan. By forcing environmental policies that disproportionately affect industries critical to these provinces' economies, Justin Trudeau has continued the legacy of regional alienation that his father began. The result has been a Canada more divided than ever, with a resurgence of Western separatism and a growing rift between urban elites and rural, working-class Canadians.

Economic Mismanagement and Corruption: A Family Tradition

If Pierre Trudeau's economic policies were disastrous for Canada's resource-based provinces, his handling of the national economy as a whole was equally problematic. Under his leadership, Canada's national debt skyrocketed, and inflation reached alarming levels. His Keynesian economic approach—relying heavily on government spending and intervention—stifled innovation and growth, leaving the country mired in debt and struggling with stagflation. Pierre's insistence on federal control over key industries, coupled with high taxation, left a lasting impact on Canada's economic trajectory.

Fast forward to Justin Trudeau's administration, and we see a similar pattern of economic mismanagement, only now compounded by allegations of corruption. The SNC-Lavalin scandal, where Justin attempted to interfere in a criminal prosecution to protect a Quebec-based company with deep ties to his government, is a glaring example of how corporate cronyism has flourished under his watch. The WE Charity scandal followed soon after, revealing that Justin's government awarded a major government contract to an organization with financial ties to his family. These scandals have eroded public trust in the Trudeau administration and exposed a government that, much like Pierre's, operates with a disregard for transparency and accountability.

Both Pierre and Justin have used their political power to favor elites—whether through the nationalization of industries that benefited Eastern Canada during Pierre's reign or through corporate favoritism in Justin's government. Meanwhile, middle- and working-class Canadians have borne the brunt of these policies, paying higher taxes and suffering through stagnant wages, inflated living costs, and job losses in industries targeted by federal overreach.

Erosion of Freedoms and National Identity

Perhaps the most insidious aspect of the Trudeau legacy has been the erosion of Canadian civil liberties and national identity. Pierre Trudeau's invocation of the War Measures Act during the October Crisis of 1970 was one of the most extreme uses of government power in Canadian history. By suspending civil liberties and deploying the military to the streets, Pierre showed a willingness to sacrifice personal freedoms in the name of national security. While many Canadians supported his decision at the time, the long-term implications of such authoritarian measures cast a shadow over his legacy as a defender of liberty.

Justin Trudeau has continued this erosion of freedoms, albeit in a different manner. His government's heavy-handed approach to regulating speech and social media, as well as the suppression of dissenting voices through media control, has created an environment where free speech is increasingly stifled. Justin's government has used taxpayer funds to subsidize mainstream media, ensuring favorable coverage while minimizing critical voices. This subtle form of censorship, combined with his embrace of identity politics, has left Canada struggling with a fractured sense of national identity. The once-proud Canadian values of personal freedom and free expression are being diluted in favor of government-imposed narratives that prioritize "correct" thinking over open debate.

The Cost of Charisma: A Country Divided

The Trudeau family's ability to maintain power, despite the damage they have inflicted, is largely due to their charismatic appeal. Pierre's intellectual bravado and Justin's media-savvy persona have allowed them to transcend their mistakes and scandals in the eyes of much of the Canadian public. But charisma cannot mask the harm they have caused. The Trudeau legacy is one of deepening regional divides, economic mismanagement, political cronyism, and an erosion of the very freedoms that Canadians once held dear.

As we delve deeper into the specifics of Pierre and Justin Trudeau's leadership, it becomes clear that their combined legacy has not been one of progress or unity, but of division, centralized control, and systemic corruption. The real question now is how much longer Canada can withstand the weight of their influence before the country fractures beyond repair.

Part I: Pierre Trudeau – The Architect of Corruption

Chapter 1: Pierre Trudeau's Ideological Roots

A Man of Contradictions

Exploring Pierre Trudeau's Background, Education, and Early Sympathies with Communist Ideologies

Pierre Elliott Trudeau, one of the most polarizing figures in Canadian history, rose to prominence as a symbol of intellectualism, progressivism, and reform. His charismatic personality, backed by a polished image of sophistication and intellect, helped cement his place as a dominant force in Canadian politics. But beneath this image lay a complex individual whose early ideological influences and sympathies with communist and socialist ideologies played a significant role in shaping his political vision and governance. Understanding Pierre's background, education, and early ideological leanings provides insight into how these formative years set the stage for his later policies, many of which centralized power, weakened provincial autonomy, and pushed Canada toward a more state-controlled system.

Pierre Trudeau's Privileged Background and Intellectual Development

Pierre Trudeau was born on October 18, 1919, into a wealthy, French-Canadian family in Montreal. His father, Charles-Émile Trudeau, was a successful businessman who made his fortune in gas stations, ensuring that young Pierre grew up in privilege and comfort. Despite the conservative, business-minded environment he was raised in, Pierre exhibited early signs of intellectual rebellion. He was highly educated, attending the prestigious Collège Jean-de-Brébeuf, a Jesuit school in Montreal, where his worldview began to expand beyond the confines of traditional Catholic education and French-Canadian nationalism.

Trudeau's formal education continued at the University of Montreal, where he earned a law degree, followed by studies at Harvard University, the London School of Economics (LSE), and the Institut d'Études Politiques in Paris. It was during these years, particularly in the late 1940s, that Trudeau's political and ideological leanings began to take shape. The intellectual climate of post-war Europe exposed Trudeau to a variety of left-wing ideologies, including socialism and Marxism, which were popular among many intellectuals and academics in the aftermath of World War II.

The London School of Economics, where Trudeau studied under Harold Laski, a prominent Marxist intellectual, had a profound impact on him. Laski advocated for state control of the economy, the redistribution of wealth, and other socialist policies— ideas that undoubtedly influenced Trudeau's thinking. Trudeau's exposure to left-wing thinkers and political movements would become a cornerstone of his intellectual development, fostering a sense of sympathy for centralized control and collective governance over individual autonomy and market-driven policies.

Pierre Trudeau's Sympathies with Communism and Socialist Ideologies

As a young man, Trudeau's intellectual curiosity and idealism drew him toward various left-wing ideologies, including socialism and communism. His travels through post-war Europe brought him into contact with a wide range of political thinkers and revolutionaries. This was particularly evident during the mid-1940s, when Trudeau visited the Soviet Union, China, and other communist countries. His travels, rather than hardening him against the brutal realities of totalitarian regimes, appeared to confirm his admiration for aspects of their centralized control and collectivist ideologies.

Trudeau's journals from his travels through China and the Soviet Union revealed a fascination with their revolutionary zeal. Despite the widespread knowledge of Stalinist purges and the brutal repression of dissent, Trudeau remained seemingly untroubled by these realities. He admired the efficiency and unity that communism ostensibly provided, even if it came at the cost of individual freedoms. His attraction to Marxist principles, particularly the idea of state-led economies and collective rights over individualism, shaped much of his thinking as he later entered politics in Canada.

Trudeau's time in China, particularly during the rise of Mao's communism, solidified his fascination with strong, centralized regimes that could mobilize populations toward nationalistic goals. Though he never fully embraced communism as a political system for Canada, his experiences left him sympathetic to certain elements of the ideology, particularly when it came to state control and planned economies. This would become evident in his policies during his time as Prime Minister, where his National Energy Program (NEP) and other federal interventions exhibited a clear preference for government regulation and control over free-market capitalism.

Aligning with Left-Wing Intellectuals and Radical Movements

Beyond his travels, Pierre Trudeau's engagement with left-wing intellectuals and radical movements also shaped his early sympathies with communism. During the 1950s and 1960s, Trudeau was part of a group of left-leaning intellectuals in Quebec known as "Les Rouges." This group, which included figures such as Gérard Pelletier and Jean Marchand, opposed the conservative, Catholic dominance of Quebec society and advocated for a more secular, progressive future for the province.

Trudeau's intellectual circle gravitated toward Marxist thought, critiquing the economic inequalities of capitalism and the influence of the Catholic Church in Quebec. They saw themselves as part of a larger global movement that sought to challenge the traditional structures of power—both religious and capitalist—and replace them with a more egalitarian society. While Trudeau's public persona as a politician would later downplay these early radical leanings, his intellectual roots in Marxist critique never fully disappeared.

In fact, throughout his political career, Trudeau maintained relationships with various left-wing figures and continued to express admiration for socialist and communist leaders around the world. His well-documented friendship with Fidel Castro, for instance, was a source of controversy throughout his time in office. While Trudeau defended his relationship with the Cuban dictator as a diplomatic necessity, it was clear that his admiration for Castro's revolutionary socialism went beyond mere statecraft. Trudeau viewed Cuba's socialist experiment as a bold and necessary response to American imperialism, reflecting his broader belief that centralized power could be a force for good, even if it required suppressing dissent and limiting individual freedoms.

Intellectual Contradictions and Political Ambitions

While Pierre Trudeau's early sympathies with communism and socialist ideologies never translated into a full-fledged embrace of these systems within Canadian politics, his intellectual contradictions were ever-present in his policies. He claimed to stand for individual liberties and freedom of expression, yet his policies, particularly the invocation of the War Measures Act during the October Crisis of 1970, showed a clear willingness to suppress civil liberties when convenient for maintaining state power.

Trudeau's belief in the central role of the state also led to policies that were fundamentally interventionist in nature. His government implemented wage and price controls, expanded social programs, and enacted sweeping federal regulations that concentrated power in Ottawa at the expense of provincial autonomy. These actions, while not overtly Marxist, were deeply rooted in the idea that the state should be the primary actor in shaping the economy and society—a principle that Trudeau likely absorbed from his early exposure to communist and socialist thinkers.

Pierre's balancing act between his public advocacy for liberal democracy and his private sympathies for authoritarian systems exemplifies the complex and often contradictory nature of his political legacy. His background, education, and early ideological leanings set the stage for a political career that was as divisive as it was transformative, leaving a legacy that continues to influence Canadian politics today.

How Pierre Trudeau's Intellectual Leanings Influenced His Political Decisions

Pierre Trudeau was a leader whose intellectual background and ideological leanings significantly shaped his political decisions and the policies he implemented during his time as Prime Minister of Canada. A deeply educated man, Trudeau's formative years studying political theory, law, and economics at elite institutions such as the University of Montreal, Harvard University, the London School of Economics, and the Sorbonne, as well as his extensive travels, exposed him to a wide range of political ideologies. Central to his intellectual formation was an engagement with socialist, Marxist, and collectivist ideas, which he absorbed from prominent thinkers and movements during his time abroad.

While Pierre Trudeau never openly declared himself a communist or socialist in the traditional sense, his policy decisions, particularly those involving state intervention and centralization of power, reflected many of the ideological tenets of these movements. His education and intellectual sympathies with left-wing thought drove his vision for a Canada that would be more centralized, regulated, and controlled by the state, rather than by individual autonomy or market forces. Understanding the influence of Trudeau's intellectual leanings is crucial to comprehending the decisions he made during his time in office, and the long-term effects of those decisions on the nation.

The London School of Economics and the Impact of Harold Laski

One of the most significant influences on Pierre Trudeau was his time at the London School of Economics (LSE), where he studied under Harold Laski, a leading Marxist political theorist and professor. Laski's ideas centered around the necessity of government control over economic resources, the redistribution of wealth, and the belief that capitalism was inherently flawed and exploitative. Laski viewed state intervention as essential to achieving equality and social justice, and these ideas resonated deeply with Trudeau.

The imprint of Laski's Marxist ideas on Trudeau's political philosophy became evident in many of the policies he enacted as Prime Minister. One of the most notable examples of this influence was Trudeau's focus on the centralization of power in Ottawa, often at the expense of provincial autonomy. Trudeau's belief that the federal government should have ultimate control over the country's economic and political systems led to the implementation of several policies that were aimed at consolidating federal power, reflecting Laski's influence.

This desire for centralized control manifested in the National Energy Program (NEP), introduced in 1980, which sought to control the oil and gas industries, key drivers of Canada's economy. The NEP was a federal attempt to redistribute resource wealth from Western provinces, particularly Alberta, to the rest of Canada, a move Trudeau justified as necessary for national economic security. This policy, however, led to significant economic downturns in the West and fueled regional resentment that still lingers today. It was an exercise in central planning reminiscent of the socialist ideas Trudeau had absorbed during his time at LSE, where the state was seen as the ultimate arbiter of economic resources.

Collectivism Over Individualism: Trudeau's Political Philosophy

Trudeau's political philosophy was deeply rooted in the belief that individual liberties could and should be subordinated to collective rights when necessary. While Trudeau publicly championed individual freedom and human rights, his actions often betrayed a belief that the state had the right to curtail these freedoms for the greater good. This notion is consistent with the Marxist idea that individual freedoms are secondary to the needs of the collective, and this philosophical stance significantly influenced many of his political decisions.

One of the clearest examples of this was his decision to invoke the War Measures Act during the October Crisis of 1970. In response to the kidnappings and violent actions of the FLQ (Front de Libération du Québec), Trudeau invoked the Act, which suspended civil liberties and gave the government sweeping powers to arrest and detain citizens without trial. The use of the military on Canadian streets and the arbitrary detainment of individuals raised serious questions about Trudeau's commitment to individual rights. When asked about the potential violation of civil liberties, Trudeau famously responded, "Just watch me." This authoritarian move reflected his intellectual belief that the needs of the state, and by extension the collective, could trump individual freedoms when deemed necessary.

Moreover, Trudeau's vision of Canadian federalism leaned heavily toward a centralized system, reducing the independence of provinces in favor of Ottawa's control. This was particularly visible in his handling of Quebec's separatist movement. While he positioned himself as a defender of national unity, his response to the Quebec sovereignty crisis showed his preference for using federal authority to suppress regional autonomy, rather than encouraging true federalist dialogue. His ideological commitment to a powerful, centralized government shaped his entire approach to governance, aligning closely with the collectivist philosophies that had influenced him in his youth.

Social Welfare Expansion: A Reflection of Socialist Ideals

Trudeau's intellectual sympathy for socialist ideologies also manifested in his expansion of Canada's social welfare system. Trudeau was a key figure in the entrenchment of social programs such as Medicare, unemployment insurance, and the Canada Pension Plan. These programs, which involved significant government intervention in the lives of Canadian citizens, were part of a broader vision of a welfare state that mirrored the socialist belief in the state's responsibility to ensure the welfare of its citizens. Trudeau believed that the federal government had a duty to manage social inequalities, even if that meant higher taxes and increased government regulation of the economy.

The expansion of the social welfare system under Trudeau was part of a larger trend toward state intervention in economic and social matters, which Trudeau saw as essential to building a just society. His policies in this area were consistent with the ideas he had absorbed during his education, where the state was seen as the guarantor of equality and social justice. While many Canadians benefited from these programs, critics argue that Trudeau's welfare state expansion increased the tax burden on individuals and businesses, stifled economic growth, and laid the groundwork for Canada's mounting national debt in the following decades.

These policies reflected a key tenet of socialism: the redistribution of wealth through government programs, funded by taxes on the affluent and successful. Trudeau's expansion of the welfare state, combined with his centralizing tendencies, can be seen as the practical application of his intellectual engagement with socialist and Marxist ideas, which advocated for reducing inequality through state intervention rather than relying on free-market mechanisms.

Trudeau's Legacy: Ideals vs. Reality

Pierre Trudeau's intellectual leanings influenced not only his policy decisions but also the long-term direction of Canada's political landscape. His affinity for centralized control, state intervention, and the curtailing of individual freedoms when necessary left a legacy of federal overreach that continues to shape Canadian politics today. His intellectual sympathies with socialist and Marxist ideas were evident in many of his policies, from the expansion of social programs to his heavy-handed use of state power during crises.

While Trudeau publicly presented himself as a defender of individual freedoms and human rights, the policies he implemented often reflected a deeper commitment to collectivist ideals. His intellectual background, steeped in the teachings of left-wing theorists like Harold Laski and shaped by his travels through communist nations, provided the philosophical foundation for his belief in a powerful, interventionist state. Though he stopped short of fully embracing communism, his policies reveal the influence of those ideologies in his approach to governance.

Ultimately, Trudeau's intellectual leanings left Canada more centralized, with a greater role for the federal government in both economic and social matters. His political decisions were not simply the product of pragmatic governance, but the culmination of years of intellectual exploration and ideological commitment to ideas that sought to reshape Canadian society, often at the expense of regional autonomy and individual freedoms.

In examining how Pierre Trudeau's intellectual leanings influenced his political decisions, it becomes clear that his education and ideological sympathies played a critical role in shaping the policies that defined his time in office. These decisions, rooted in a belief in the centrality of the state, have left a lasting impact on Canada, for better or worse.

Chapter 2: Trudeau's Ties with Dictators

Trudeau's Close Relationship with Fidel Castro and His Public Admiration for Communist Regimes

One of the most controversial aspects of Pierre Trudeau's political career was his close relationship with Fidel Castro and his broader public admiration for communist regimes. While Trudeau positioned himself as a champion of democracy and human rights in Canada, his personal and political connections to leaders of authoritarian regimes, particularly in the communist world, painted a more complex—and for many, contradictory—picture. Pierre Trudeau's friendship with Fidel Castro, in particular, exemplified his ideological sympathy for the centralized control and collectivist principles espoused by communist regimes, even as these regimes were responsible for suppressing freedoms and violating human rights.

Trudeau's affinity for leftist dictatorships was not an isolated quirk of his personality but rather an extension of his intellectual leanings, formed during his early years of education and travel. This ideological sympathy had a tangible impact on his foreign policy, as well as on his legacy as a leader who, despite his democratic rhetoric, appeared to have an unusual comfort with authoritarian governance models.

The Friendship with Fidel Castro: A Personal and Political Connection

Pierre Trudeau's relationship with Fidel Castro, the communist revolutionary and long-time leader of Cuba, has been a subject of intrigue and controversy. Trudeau first visited Cuba in 1976, becoming the first NATO leader to do so, despite the ongoing Cold War tensions between the Western world and the communist bloc. The visit was more than just a diplomatic gesture; it was the beginning of a personal friendship between Trudeau and Castro that would last for decades. During his time in Cuba, Trudeau famously declared, "Viva Cuba! Viva Fidel Castro!"—a public expression of solidarity with Castro's regime, which was particularly striking given Castro's role as a dictator who had violently overthrown the previous government and established a one-party communist state.

For Trudeau, Castro's Cuba represented a socialist experiment that aligned with some of his own ideological leanings, particularly the emphasis on state control over the economy and the rejection of Western capitalist imperialism. Despite Castro's brutal repression of political dissent, his curtailing of free speech, and the lack of democratic elections in Cuba, Trudeau publicly praised the regime for its accomplishments, such as universal healthcare and education. He viewed Cuba as a counterweight to American influence in the region, and his open admiration for Castro's leadership was seen as a bold and provocative stance at the time.

This friendship extended beyond Trudeau's time in office. Even after leaving political life, Trudeau maintained contact with Castro, and the two continued to express mutual respect. When Pierre Trudeau died in 2000, Castro was one of the few world leaders invited to attend his funeral in Canada. Castro not only attended but also served as an honorary pallbearer, a testament to the deep personal bond that had formed between the two men. The sight of the communist dictator at the funeral of a Western democratic leader highlighted the odd juxtaposition of Trudeau's public advocacy for democracy and his private comfort with authoritarian regimes.

Public Admiration for Communist Regimes: Beyond Cuba

Trudeau's admiration for communist regimes extended beyond Cuba, as he cultivated relationships with other leaders of authoritarian left-wing governments. During his formative years, Trudeau traveled extensively through the Soviet Union and China, two of the most prominent communist states in the world at the time. While many Western leaders viewed these regimes with suspicion, Trudeau seemed intrigued by their revolutionary zeal and their rejection of capitalist and imperialist systems. His writings from these trips revealed a complex mix of admiration and critique, but it was clear that Trudeau saw value in the centralized control and collective ethos promoted by communist ideologies.

In 1960, long before becoming Prime Minister, Trudeau traveled to China, then under the rule of Mao Zedong. Mao's regime was in the midst of the disastrous Great Leap Forward, a campaign that led to widespread famine and the deaths of millions. However, Trudeau's reflections on his time in China largely glossed over these atrocities, focusing instead on the positive aspects of the communist experiment, particularly the sense of collective purpose and national unity he observed. This selective admiration for the successes of communist regimes while ignoring their human rights abuses became a recurring theme in Trudeau's approach to foreign affairs.

Similarly, Trudeau visited the Soviet Union in 1952, during the height of Joseph Stalin's rule. While much of the Western world was focused on the Cold War and the oppressive nature of the Soviet regime, Trudeau's writings from his trip were strikingly uncritical. He expressed fascination with the Soviet system and showed little concern for the repression and purges that were occurring under Stalin's leadership. For Trudeau, the Soviet Union represented an alternative model to Western democracy and capitalism, one that was worth studying, even if he did not fully endorse it.

Trudeau's public praise for aspects of these regimes, particularly their state-driven economies and social reforms, contrasted sharply with the values of liberal democracy that he purported to champion in Canada. While he never openly advocated for communism in Canada, his admiration for the organizational strength and revolutionary spirit of these regimes was evident. This ideological sympathy likely influenced some of his domestic policies, particularly his preference for centralization and state intervention in the economy.

Influence on Trudeau's Foreign Policy: Ideology Meets Pragmatism

Trudeau's admiration for communist regimes had a significant impact on his foreign policy decisions as Prime Minister. While he maintained Canada's position as part of the Western democratic alliance, particularly through its membership in NATO, Trudeau often pursued a more independent and sometimes controversial approach to international relations. His foreign policy was characterized by a desire to distance Canada from American influence and to engage with countries that were often seen as adversaries by the West.

This was most evident in his approach to Cuba. While the United States maintained a strict embargo and severed diplomatic ties with the Castro regime, Trudeau strengthened Canada's relationship with Cuba, advocating for normalized relations and economic cooperation. His decision to engage with Cuba, rather than isolate it, was in line with his broader belief that Canada should assert its own foreign policy, free from the dictates of its southern neighbor.

Trudeau's relationships with other communist leaders, such as Mao Zedong and Soviet Premier Leonid

Brezhnev, also reflected his willingness to engage with regimes that were ideologically opposed to Western liberal democracy. In 1971, Trudeau made a historic trip to the Soviet Union, where he met with Brezhnev to discuss issues of global peace and trade. While these diplomatic efforts were framed as pragmatic, they were also consistent with Trudeau's ideological belief that Canada should not blindly follow the Western bloc in its Cold War hostilities.

At the same time, Trudeau's foreign policy often appeared hypocritical to his critics, who pointed out the contradiction between his public defense of human rights and his cozy relationships with dictators like Castro. Trudeau's supporters argued that his engagement with communist regimes was pragmatic and necessary for global peace, but his personal admiration for these leaders raised questions about the true extent of his ideological sympathies.

The Legacy of Trudeau's Relationship with Communist Regimes

The close relationship between Pierre Trudeau and Fidel Castro, as well as Trudeau's broader admiration for communist regimes, has left a lasting mark on his legacy. For many, it is difficult to reconcile Trudeau's domestic image as a defender of liberal democracy with his fondness for authoritarian leaders abroad. His friendship with Castro, in particular, remains a point of contention in Canadian political discourse, with some viewing it as a bold stance against American imperialism, while others see it as a betrayal of democratic values.

Moreover, Trudeau's engagement with communist regimes set a precedent for Canadian foreign policy that was independent of American influence, but it also opened the door to criticism that Canada under Trudeau was too willing to overlook human rights abuses in pursuit of ideological alignment and economic opportunity. His legacy in this regard is one of complexity—a leader who, while never abandoning democratic principles at home, showed a troubling affinity for authoritarian systems abroad.

Pierre Trudeau's close relationship with Fidel Castro and his public admiration for communist regimes were defining elements of his political career. While Trudeau presented himself as a staunch defender of democratic freedoms and human rights at home, his affinity for leaders like Castro, Mao, and Brezhnev revealed a more complex ideological stance. Trudeau admired the revolutionary spirit and centralized control of communist regimes, even as he distanced himself from their more brutal authoritarian tactics. His foreign policy reflected a desire to position Canada as an independent player on the world stage, free from the influence of the United States, but it also raised questions about his commitment to democratic values when engaging with authoritarian states.

In the end, Trudeau's legacy is one of contradictions. He was a leader who fought for individual rights and freedoms in Canada, yet maintained deep friendships with dictators who ruled through oppression. His public admiration for these regimes has left a lasting impact on how he is remembered—a symbol of both progress and pragmatism, but also of ideological inconsistency.

The Ethical Implications of Supporting a Dictatorship While Promoting Himself as a Defender of Freedom

One of the most enduring and perplexing aspects of Pierre Trudeau's political career is the contrast between his public persona as a champion of democracy, human rights, and individual freedoms, and his personal admiration for, and relationships with, authoritarian regimes—most notably his friendship with Fidel Castro and his support for various communist leaders. This paradox raises profound ethical questions about Trudeau's legacy, his consistency as a political leader, and the principles that guided his foreign policy decisions.

On the one hand, Trudeau is remembered for his contributions to liberal democracy in Canada, including the implementation of the Charter of Rights and Freedoms in 1982, which enshrined civil liberties and personal freedoms in Canadian law. On the other hand, his close relationships with leaders of undemocratic regimes, who systematically suppressed these very freedoms, created a fundamental contradiction in his political philosophy and leadership. The ethical implications of these dual allegiances reveal a complex, and at times, morally inconsistent leader who navigated the murky waters of international diplomacy and ideology.

The Contradiction: Champion of Rights, Friend of Dictators

At home, Pierre Trudeau built a reputation as a progressive reformer. He pushed for greater civil liberties, fought against regional divisions, and worked to entrench protections for minorities, individual rights, and personal freedoms. His advocacy for equality and justice was a hallmark of his domestic policies, culminating in the 1982 Constitution Act and the Charter of Rights and Freedoms, which remain cornerstones of Canada's legal framework for protecting individual rights.

However, this commitment to democratic values appeared to falter when it came to Trudeau's international relationships—most notably his enthusiastic support of Fidel Castro's dictatorship in Cuba. Trudeau's close friendship with Castro, despite Cuba's well-documented human rights abuses, suppression of free speech, and imprisonment of political dissidents, seemed to contradict his stated belief in human dignity and freedom. While Trudeau defended his friendship with Castro as a pragmatic diplomatic decision, the ethical concerns surrounding this relationship cannot be ignored.

Fidel Castro ruled Cuba with an iron fist, silencing opposition, censoring the press, and eliminating political pluralism. Under Castro's rule, Cuba became a one-party state where dissent was not tolerated. For Trudeau, a leader who preached democratic ideals, to openly support and admire such a regime raises serious ethical questions. How could Trudeau reconcile his admiration for Castro's revolution with his commitment to the rights and freedoms of individuals? How could a self-proclaimed defender of freedom justify close ties with a leader who systematically violated the very principles Trudeau championed in Canada?

Moral Relativism in International Relations

One possible explanation for Trudeau's stance lies in the realm of moral relativism, particularly in the context of Cold War diplomacy. Trudeau, like many Western leaders during this period, operated in a world defined by two ideological extremes: Western capitalism, led by the United States, and Soviet-style communism, represented by the USSR and its satellite states, including Cuba. While the Western narrative often framed the Cold War as a battle between freedom and totalitarianism, Trudeau adopted a more nuanced, morally relativistic approach.

Trudeau's foreign policy sought to distance Canada from the United States' interventionist approach to Latin America and its hardline stance against communism. In this context, Trudeau may have viewed Castro not as a brutal dictator but as a revolutionary leader resisting American imperialism. Trudeau's admiration for Castro and Cuba was likely rooted in the perception that the revolution had succeeded in building a society that rejected the inequalities and exploitation associated with capitalist systems. In this light, Trudeau's support for Castro could be seen as an extension of his opposition to American hegemony, rather than an endorsement of Castro's authoritarianism.

However, this morally relativistic stance poses significant ethical problems. By excusing or overlooking the repressive aspects of Castro's rule, Trudeau effectively engaged in a form of ethical doublethink. He framed his support for Castro as solidarity with a nation resisting Western domination, but in doing so, he ignored the human cost of that revolution—the lives destroyed by political repression, the voices silenced by a dictatorship, and the freedoms denied to the Cuban people. In the process, Trudeau's ethical principles became flexible, depending on the geopolitical context.

Hypocrisy and Selective Morality

The ethical implications of Trudeau's relationships with authoritarian regimes extend beyond Castro and Cuba. His visits to China during Mao Zedong's reign and the Soviet Union under Stalin and Khrushchev further illustrate his willingness to engage with some of the world's most repressive regimes, all while promoting himself as a champion of freedom and democracy at home. In the case of Mao's China, Trudeau downplayed the atrocities of the Great Leap Forward and the Cultural Revolution, which resulted in the deaths of millions of people and the destruction of countless lives. His focus, instead, was on the revolutionary achievements of the Chinese Communist Party, such as land reform and industrial development.

This selective morality—whereby Trudeau praised certain aspects of communist regimes while ignoring their glaring human rights abuses—raises significant ethical concerns. It suggests that Trudeau was willing to overlook profound injustices when they aligned with his broader geopolitical goals or ideological sympathies. This form of ethical flexibility can be seen as a form of hypocrisy, where Trudeau's moral principles were applied selectively based on political expediency rather than consistent adherence to the values of freedom and human rights.

For many of Trudeau's critics, this inconsistency was deeply troubling. By aligning himself with dictators like Castro and downplaying the repressive nature of communist regimes, Trudeau undermined his credibility as a defender of freedom. His actions sent a message that human rights and individual freedoms were negotiable in the realm of international politics, and that authoritarianism could be tolerated—or even admired— if it served broader ideological purposes.

The Consequences for Canada's International Reputation

Trudeau's support for authoritarian regimes had broader ethical implications for Canada's international standing.

Canada has long prided itself on its role as a middle power, promoting peace, democracy, and human rights around the world. Yet, Trudeau's relationships with dictatorships risked tarnishing that reputation, suggesting that Canada's commitment to these values was conditional. By maintaining close ties with leaders like Castro, Trudeau opened Canada to accusations of hypocrisy on the global stage.

Moreover, Trudeau's foreign policy choices complicated Canada's relationships with other democratic nations, particularly the United States. While Trudeau sought to distinguish Canada's foreign policy from that of its southern neighbor, his engagement with dictatorships raised ethical concerns about the extent to which Canada was willing to prioritize its moral values over geopolitical strategy. This balancing act—attempting to engage with both democratic allies and authoritarian regimes—left Canada's foreign policy vulnerable to charges of inconsistency and opportunism.

The Legacy of Ethical Contradictions

Pierre Trudeau's legacy as a defender of freedom is undoubtedly complex, particularly when weighed against his personal and political relationships with authoritarian leaders like Fidel Castro. While Trudeau made significant contributions to enshrining individual rights and freedoms in Canada, his admiration for and support of dictatorial regimes abroad revealed a troubling inconsistency in his ethical framework. The ethical implications of this contradiction—supporting dictatorships while promoting himself as a defender of freedom—continue to provoke debate and shape perceptions of Trudeau's legacy.

In the end, Trudeau's foreign policy and personal relationships raise profound ethical questions about the responsibilities of democratic leaders in the international arena. Is it ever justifiable to engage with authoritarian regimes in the pursuit of broader political goals? Can a leader truly claim to be a defender of freedom if they are willing to overlook the human rights abuses of their allies? These are the questions that Pierre Trudeau's career forces us to confront, and they remain as relevant today as they were during his time in office.

Pierre Trudeau's dual roles as a domestic champion of freedom and an international admirer of authoritarian regimes present a complex and ethically challenging legacy. His close friendship with Fidel Castro and his broader support for communist dictatorships stand in stark contrast to his public commitment to democratic values. This contradiction raises important ethical questions about the nature of political alliances, moral consistency, and the cost of realpolitik in a world divided by ideological conflicts.

Ultimately, Trudeau's legacy forces us to grapple with the uncomfortable reality that even leaders who advocate for freedom and democracy can, at times, be complicit in supporting regimes that suppress these very principles. The ethical implications of Trudeau's choices continue to resonate, reminding us that the ideals of freedom and human rights must be upheld consistently if they are to have any real meaning.

Chapter 3: Economic Sabotage and Corruption

How Pierre Trudeau's National Energy Program (NEP) Devastated the Canadian Economy, Especially in Western Canada, to Centralize Power in Ottawa

Pierre Trudeau's National Energy Program (NEP), introduced in 1980, is one of the most infamous and contentious economic policies in Canadian history. Ostensibly designed to secure Canada's energy independence and shield Canadians from rising global oil prices, the NEP instead devastated the Canadian economy, particularly in Western Canada, where the energy sector was vital to regional prosperity. The program not only caused economic turmoil but also exacerbated regional divisions and furthered a longstanding tension between the federal government in Ottawa and the provinces, particularly Alberta.

Critics argue that the NEP was not just a misguided economic policy, but a deliberate attempt by Trudeau's Liberal government to centralize power in Ottawa at the expense of provincial autonomy, especially in energy-rich Western Canada. Through mechanisms of federal control over natural resources and redistributive policies, the NEP drained wealth from the West to benefit the federal government and its supporters in Eastern Canada. The political, economic, and social ramifications of this policy continue to reverberate in Canadian politics today.

The Goals of the National Energy Program

In the late 1970s, the world experienced a sharp increase in oil prices due to the OPEC oil embargo and the Iranian Revolution. For oil-producing countries, including Canada, this price surge presented an opportunity for windfall profits. However, the Trudeau government, wary of rising energy costs for Canadians, decided to intervene in the oil market through the NEP, announced in the October 1980 federal budget.

The stated goals of the NEP were threefold:

1. To achieve Canadian energy self-sufficiency.
2. To increase federal revenue from energy production.
3. To redistribute wealth from the oil-rich provinces to the rest of Canada.

Under the NEP, the federal government imposed new taxes on oil production, implemented price controls on domestically produced oil, and offered incentives to Canadian-owned oil companies to promote Canadian ownership of the energy sector. While these measures were intended to protect Canadian consumers from rising global oil prices and reduce dependence on foreign energy, they came at a steep cost to oil-producing provinces, particularly Alberta.

The Economic Devastation in Western Canada

The NEP disproportionately affected Alberta, where the oil and gas industry was the backbone of the economy. The program imposed significant federal controls on oil production and pricing, effectively capping the price that Canadian producers could charge for oil. This was far below the market price, which meant that oil companies in Alberta were forced to sell their product at artificially low rates. The federal government justified these price controls as necessary to protect Canadian consumers, but in reality, they were seen as a means of transferring wealth from Alberta to Ottawa.

Additionally, the NEP introduced a new federal tax on oil revenues, which further reduced the profits of oil producers. This tax siphoned billions of dollars out of Alberta's economy and redirected it to the federal government, which used the funds to subsidize energy projects in other parts of the country, particularly in Eastern Canada. This redistribution of wealth was perceived by many in Alberta as a federal overreach, an attempt by Ottawa to take advantage of the province's natural resources for the benefit of the central government and its political allies in Ontario and Quebec.

The economic impact of the NEP in Alberta was severe. Oil companies, both domestic and foreign, drastically reduced their investment in the province, leading to job losses, economic stagnation, and a sharp decline in provincial revenue. Many companies abandoned planned projects due to the unprofitable nature of the industry under the NEP's price controls and taxation regime. Alberta, which had been experiencing rapid growth and prosperity due to its energy sector, suddenly found itself in the midst of an economic downturn. The sense of betrayal and resentment toward Ottawa grew as Alberta's economy suffered while the federal government continued to impose policies that benefited other parts of the country.

Centralizing Power in Ottawa

While the economic impacts of the NEP were devastating, the political ramifications were equally profound. The NEP represented an unprecedented federal intervention in what had traditionally been a provincial jurisdiction—natural resources. Under the Canadian Constitution, provinces have control over their own natural resources, and the oil and gas industry in Alberta had long been a source of provincial pride and autonomy. However, the NEP essentially overruled provincial control by imposing federal regulations and taxation on the oil industry, allowing Ottawa to take a significant share of Alberta's oil revenue.

This centralization of power in Ottawa was seen by many in Western Canada as an attack on provincial rights. Alberta, which had long felt marginalized by the federal government, particularly under Pierre Trudeau's leadership, viewed the NEP as an assault on its economic independence. The resentment toward Ottawa, which had been simmering for years, boiled over during the implementation of the NEP. Alberta Premier Peter Lougheed led the charge against the NEP, arguing that it violated the constitutional rights of provinces to manage their own resources and accusing the federal government of exploiting Alberta's wealth to fund its own political agenda in Eastern Canada.

The NEP also exacerbated existing tensions between Alberta and Quebec, the latter of which was perceived as receiving preferential treatment from the federal government under Trudeau's leadership. While Alberta's oil revenues were being taxed to support national energy projects, Quebec continued to benefit from federal equalization payments and other subsidies. This created a deep sense of unfairness in Alberta and other Western provinces, fueling a broader sentiment of Western alienation—a belief that the federal government in Ottawa prioritized the interests of Eastern Canada over those of the West.

The Lasting Legacy of the NEP

The NEP was ultimately short-lived, ending with the election of Brian Mulroney's Progressive Conservative government in 1984. Mulroney, recognizing the deep divisions caused by the NEP, quickly dismantled the program and sought to repair relations with Western Canada. However, the economic and political damage caused by the NEP left a lasting legacy. Alberta's economy took years to recover from the shock of the NEP, and the program became a symbol of federal overreach and Eastern Canada's exploitation of Western resources.

The resentment toward Ottawa that the NEP sparked did not fade with the program's end. Instead, it solidified a sense of Western alienation that continues to influence Canadian politics today. In Alberta, the NEP became a rallying cry for politicians advocating for greater provincial autonomy and even for separatist movements that called for Alberta to secede from Canada. The bitterness over the NEP was passed down through generations, shaping Alberta's political identity and its relationship with the federal government.

The NEP also reinforced the idea that Ottawa, under Pierre Trudeau's leadership, sought to centralize power at the expense of provincial rights. Trudeau's broader legacy of federal intervention and his disregard for Western concerns left a deep scar on Canada's political landscape, contributing to the rise of movements like Western alienation and provincial sovereignty that persist to this day.

Pierre Trudeau's National Energy Program was more than just an economic policy—it was a deliberate attempt to centralize power in Ottawa and redistribute wealth from Alberta to the federal government. While the NEP was framed as a national effort to protect Canadians from rising energy costs and secure energy independence, its true impact was the economic devastation of Alberta and the deepening of regional divisions. By overriding provincial control of natural resources and imposing federal taxes on oil production, the NEP represented a federal power grab that left Western Canada feeling exploited and marginalized.

The political and economic consequences of the NEP continue to shape Canada's national discourse, with Western alienation and calls for greater provincial autonomy remaining central issues in Canadian politics. Trudeau's legacy in Western Canada is still defined by the NEP, a policy that many view as an example of how Ottawa prioritized the interests of Eastern Canada over the West and centralized power at the expense of provincial autonomy.

Allegations of Cronyism and Favoritism Toward Eastern Canadian Interests in Pierre Trudeau's National Energy Program (NEP)

Pierre Trudeau's National Energy Program (NEP) not only devastated the economy of Western Canada but also sparked deep-seated allegations of cronyism and favoritism toward Eastern Canadian interests, particularly those of Quebec and Ontario. Introduced in 1980, the NEP was seen by many as a tool to redistribute wealth from resource-rich provinces like Alberta to the federal government and its political base in Eastern Canada. Critics argue that the program was less about securing Canada's energy independence and more about centralizing power in Ottawa while benefiting Trudeau's political allies and economic supporters in Quebec and Ontario. These accusations of favoritism and cronyism continue to fuel the deep divide between Western and

Eastern Canada, a legacy that persists in Canadian politics today.

Eastern Canadian Interests: The Political Context of the NEP

To understand the allegations of cronyism and favoritism, it is essential to view the NEP within the broader political context of the time. Pierre Trudeau's Liberal Party had its strongest support base in Quebec and Ontario, the two most populous provinces in Canada. The Liberals had historically struggled to gain significant traction in Western Canada, where the Conservative Party and regional interests dominated. This regional divide in political support was a critical factor in the formulation and implementation of the NEP, as Trudeau's government sought to solidify its hold on Eastern Canada by catering to the economic and political interests of its supporters in these provinces.

The NEP was framed as a national policy designed to protect Canadian consumers from rising global oil prices and ensure energy independence. However, many critics argue that it was, in reality, a political maneuver to appease Eastern Canadian voters at the expense of Western provinces, particularly Alberta. By imposing taxes and price controls on Alberta's oil industry, the NEP effectively redistributed wealth from the West to the federal government, which then used those funds to support national energy projects and programs that disproportionately benefited Eastern Canada.

Allegations of Cronyism: Quebec's Favored Position

One of the most persistent allegations surrounding the NEP is that it was designed to benefit Quebec at the expense of Western Canada. Pierre Trudeau, a proud Quebecer, had a vested interest in maintaining political support in his home province, particularly in the face of rising Quebec separatism during the late 1970s and early 1980s. The NEP, many argue, was a way to ensure that the economic benefits of Canada's energy wealth were funneled toward Quebec, shoring up political support for the federalist cause and securing Trudeau's electoral base.

Under the NEP, the federal government used revenue generated from Alberta's oil production to subsidize energy projects and industries in Eastern Canada, particularly in Quebec. One example of this was the Petro-Canada initiative, a government-owned oil company that was heavily promoted and supported by the Trudeau government as part of the NEP. Critics argue that Petro-Canada was used as a vehicle to channel federal investment into Quebec's economy, creating jobs and supporting industrial growth in the province while Alberta bore the financial burden.

This perception of favoritism was not limited to Quebec. Ontario, Canada's manufacturing heartland, also benefited from the NEP through lower energy prices and federal investment in national energy infrastructure. The NEP's price controls on oil disproportionately benefited consumers and industries in Ontario and Quebec, where lower energy costs were critical to maintaining economic stability. Meanwhile, Alberta, which relied on oil revenues to fund its own economy, saw its profits shrink under the NEP's taxation and pricing policies.

The Business Connection: Liberal Cronyism and Corporate Favoritism

Another dimension of the cronyism allegations tied to the NEP was the belief that Trudeau's government was using the program to reward its corporate allies, particularly those based in Eastern Canada. The federal incentives for Canadian-owned oil companies under the NEP raised suspicions that the policy was designed to benefit certain well-connected businesses with ties to the Liberal Party, furthering their dominance in the energy sector. By promoting Canadian ownership of the energy industry, the NEP funneled government support toward businesses that were aligned with the Liberal government, particularly in Quebec and Ontario.

The creation of Petro-Canada itself was seen by many as a vehicle for federal control over the oil industry, with critics accusing the Trudeau government of using the state-owned enterprise to cement its political and economic influence in Quebec. Moreover, the appointment of political insiders and allies to leadership positions within Petro-Canada and other government-related energy projects reinforced the perception that the NEP was less about energy independence and more about ensuring that federal resources were directed toward Liberal-aligned interests.

The NEP's emphasis on Canadian ownership of oil resources also created an environment where Eastern Canadian companies were favored for government contracts and investment, while foreign and Western Canadian oil firms were marginalized. This created further resentment in Alberta, where many oil companies were either foreign-owned or Western-based, and saw the NEP as an attack on their ability to compete and grow. The program was perceived as a way to weaken Alberta's influence in the energy sector and centralize control in Ottawa, where Eastern interests held more sway.

The Political Fallout: Widening the East-West Divide

The economic and political fallout from the NEP only served to deepen the existing regional divide between Western and Eastern Canada. Alberta, which had been experiencing an economic boom due to its oil industry, suddenly found itself in the midst of a severe economic downturn as the NEP's price controls and taxes drained the province's revenue. Job losses, reduced investment, and economic stagnation followed, leaving many Albertans feeling that Ottawa had deliberately targeted their province to benefit the political and economic elites in Quebec and Ontario.

This sense of betrayal was compounded by the perception that the NEP was designed to prop up Trudeau's political base in Eastern Canada, where the Liberal Party drew most of its support. The NEP became a symbol of federal overreach and Eastern dominance, reinforcing the belief in Western Canada that Ottawa and Eastern Canada were more concerned with protecting their own interests than with ensuring equitable economic opportunities for all Canadians. This perception of favoritism and cronyism sparked a wave of political activism in Alberta, with calls for greater provincial autonomy and, in some cases, outright separatism.

The political legacy of the NEP continues to influence Canadian politics today. Western alienation, a term used to describe the feeling of political and economic disenfranchisement in Western Canada, remains a powerful force in Alberta and other Western provinces. The NEP is often cited as the catalyst for this movement, as it demonstrated, in the eyes of many Western Canadians, the lengths to which Ottawa was willing to go to centralize power and favor its political allies in Eastern Canada.

Pierre Trudeau's National Energy Program was a deeply divisive policy that not only devastated Alberta's economy but also exacerbated longstanding regional tensions between Western and Eastern Canada. The allegations of cronyism and favoritism that surrounded the NEP reflect the broader perception that the program was designed to benefit the political and economic elites in Quebec and Ontario, at the expense of Western Canada's prosperity. By redistributing wealth from the West to the federal government and promoting Canadian ownership of the energy sector, the NEP served as a vehicle for centralizing power in Ottawa and rewarding Trudeau's political allies.

The NEP's legacy is one of political and economic division, with Western Canada still grappling with the aftereffects of a policy that many see as an example of federal overreach and favoritism. For many Western Canadians, the NEP remains a symbol of how Ottawa, under Trudeau's leadership, prioritized the interests of Eastern Canada while marginalizing the economic and political rights of the West—a division that continues to shape Canadian politics to this day.

Chapter 4: Civil Liberties Under Attack

Trudeau's Handling of the FLQ Crisis and His Decision to Invoke the War Measures Act: Suspending Civil Liberties Across Canada

Pierre Trudeau's handling of the October Crisis in 1970 is one of the most controversial episodes of his time as Prime Minister, as it directly challenged Canada's commitment to civil liberties and the rule of law. Faced with a surge of domestic terrorism by the Front de Libération du Québec (FLQ), a militant Quebec separatist group, Trudeau made the unprecedented decision to invoke the War Measures Act, effectively suspending civil liberties across the country. This decision allowed for mass arrests, the use of military force within Canadian borders, and the suppression of political dissent under the guise of national security. For many, this marked a moment when Trudeau's image as a progressive leader committed to civil rights was fundamentally called into question.

The decision to invoke the War Measures Act was not only controversial for its immediate impact but also for the broader ethical and political implications it carried. It raised questions about the balance between security and freedom, the limits of government power, and the long-term consequences of using extraordinary measures to combat internal threats. Trudeau's actions during the October Crisis continue to be a point of debate, symbolizing both his strong-handed approach to governance and his willingness to prioritize state control over individual rights when confronted with a national emergency.

Background: The Rise of the FLQ and the October Crisis

The Front de Libération du Québec (FLQ) was a radical Quebec separatist group that emerged in the 1960s, advocating for Quebec's independence from Canada through violent means. The group was responsible for a series of bombings, kidnappings, and other acts of terrorism aimed at both the federal government and symbols of Anglophone dominance in Quebec. Their ultimate goal was to establish an independent, socialist Quebec free from federal control.

By 1970, the FLQ had grown increasingly bold in its actions. On October 5, 1970, they kidnapped British diplomat James Cross from his residence in Montreal, demanding the release of imprisoned FLQ members in exchange for his life. Five days later, they escalated their campaign by kidnapping Quebec Minister of Labour Pierre Laporte. These kidnappings shocked the nation and plunged Quebec into a state of fear and uncertainty. The FLQ's demands were not only political but also symbolic, representing the growing frustration among Quebec's separatist movement with what they perceived as federal oppression.

As tensions escalated, the Quebec provincial government, led by Premier Robert Bourassa, requested federal assistance in dealing with the crisis. In response,

Pierre Trudeau made the controversial decision to invoke the War Measures Act on October 16, 1970, effectively granting the federal government extraordinary powers to address the crisis. This was the first and only time in Canadian history that the War Measures Act was invoked during peacetime.

The War Measures Act: Suspending Civil Liberties

The War Measures Act, originally enacted during World War I, gave the federal government sweeping powers to preserve national security during times of war or insurrection. Its invocation in 1970 granted the Trudeau government extraordinary authority to detain individuals without charge, restrict freedom of movement, impose censorship, and deploy military forces in civilian areas. In effect, the War Measures Act suspended many of the civil liberties guaranteed by the Canadian Bill of Rights, including the right to habeas corpus (protection against arbitrary detention).

Once the Act was invoked, Canadian military forces were deployed in Quebec, and the police were granted the power to arrest and detain individuals suspected of being connected to the FLQ or its activities. Over 450 people were arrested during the crackdown, most without any formal charges or evidence of involvement in terrorist activities. These individuals included political activists, intellectuals, and community leaders who had no proven links to the FLQ but were vocal supporters of Quebec sovereignty. In this atmosphere of fear and suspicion, civil liberties were curtailed, and dissent was swiftly suppressed.

Trudeau's response to critics of his decision to invoke the War Measures Act was famously defiant. In a television interview, when asked how far he was willing to go to maintain law and order, Trudeau responded with the now-infamous phrase, "Just watch me." This declaration was seen by many as a reflection of Trudeau's willingness to use the full force of state power to crush the FLQ and prevent the spread of violence. However, it also came to symbolize the authoritarian tendencies in Trudeau's governance, where civil rights and individual freedoms were sacrificed in the name of national security.

The Ethical and Legal Implications of Invoking the War Measures Act

The decision to invoke the War Measures Act and the resulting suspension of civil liberties raised profound ethical and legal questions about the limits of government power in a democracy. While Trudeau justified the use of the Act as necessary to preserve national security and prevent further acts of terrorism, the broad scope of the powers it granted—particularly the detention of individuals without due process—was widely criticized as an overreach of state authority.

The mass arrests of political activists and intellectuals who had no connection to the FLQ's violent activities underscored the dangers of such unchecked power.

Many of those arrested were detained simply for their political beliefs or for their support of Quebec nationalism, not for any involvement in terrorist activities. This widespread targeting of political dissenters led to accusations that the Trudeau government was using the FLQ crisis as a pretext to crack down on the broader Quebec sovereignty movement.

Civil libertarians, human rights advocates, and political commentators condemned the use of the War Measures Act as a violation of fundamental democratic principles. They argued that the suspension of civil liberties set a dangerous precedent, where the government could invoke emergency powers to suppress political opposition under the guise of maintaining security. The fact that the FLQ crisis, while serious, did not represent an existential threat to the Canadian state only heightened concerns that Trudeau's response was disproportionate and authoritarian.

The use of the War Measures Act also had long-lasting consequences for how Canadians viewed the balance between security and freedom. While many Canadians initially supported Trudeau's actions—believing that the situation in Quebec warranted extraordinary measures—there was growing discomfort in the years that followed over the extent of the government's crackdown and its impact on civil rights. The legacy of the October Crisis remains a touchstone in Canadian political discourse, raising questions about how far a democratic government should go in curtailing rights in times of crisis.

Centralization of Power and Political Control

Beyond the immediate ethical concerns surrounding the suspension of civil liberties, the invocation of the War Measures Act had broader political implications related to Trudeau's efforts to centralize power in Ottawa. Throughout his political career, Trudeau was an advocate of strong federal control, often at the expense of provincial autonomy. His decision to invoke the War Measures Act in Quebec, a province with a long history of advocating for greater autonomy and even independence, reinforced the perception that Trudeau was willing to use federal power to suppress regional dissent.

For Quebec nationalists, the War Measures Act became a symbol of Ottawa's disregard for Quebec's unique cultural and political aspirations. While the FLQ represented only a small, militant faction of the larger sovereignty movement, Trudeau's decision to use military force and mass arrests against Quebecers, many of whom were innocent, deepened the province's sense of alienation from the rest of Canada. This contributed to the rise of the Parti Québécois, a political party committed to Quebec's independence, which would later lead the province through two referendums on sovereignty.

From a broader national perspective, the October Crisis also raised concerns about the centralization of executive power in times of crisis. Trudeau's use of the War Measures Act demonstrated how easily a government could override civil liberties and the rule of law in the name of security, setting a precedent that could be exploited by future governments facing domestic unrest. This centralization of power was a recurring theme in Trudeau's governance, and the October Crisis highlighted the extent to which he was willing to prioritize state control over individual freedoms.

Pierre Trudeau's decision to invoke the War Measures Act during the October Crisis remains one of the most controversial moments of his tenure as Prime Minister. While the immediate threat posed by the FLQ was serious, the use of extraordinary powers to suspend civil liberties across Canada raised profound ethical and legal concerns about the limits of government authority in a democracy. The mass arrests, the deployment of military forces, and the targeting of political dissenters reflected a willingness to sacrifice individual rights in the name of national security—an approach that left a lasting legacy on Canadian politics and civil liberties.

For many Canadians, the October Crisis exposed the dangers of granting the federal government unchecked power, particularly in moments of national crisis. The ethical implications of Trudeau's actions continue to resonate today, as Canadians grapple with the balance between security and freedom in the face of modern challenges. The invocation of the War Measures Act remains a powerful reminder of how easily civil liberties can be curtailed, and how the centralization of power can undermine the very democratic values that a government is sworn to protect.

The Use of Heavy-Handed Government Tactics to Silence Political Dissent Under the Guise of National Security: Trudeau and the October Crisis

Pierre Trudeau's handling of the October Crisis in 1970, particularly his decision to invoke the War Measures Act, is a clear example of how heavy-handed government tactics can be used to silence political dissent under the guise of maintaining national security. Faced with a growing separatist movement in Quebec and the militant actions of the Front de Libération du Québec (FLQ), Trudeau responded with an unprecedented suspension of civil liberties across Canada. This approach raised serious concerns about the abuse of state power, as the government not only targeted the violent elements of the FLQ but also used the crisis as an opportunity to suppress broader political dissent in Quebec.

Trudeau's actions during the October Crisis exposed a darker side of his leadership—his willingness to prioritize state control and suppress opposition when challenged by internal threats. By invoking the War Measures Act, Trudeau granted the federal government sweeping powers, which included mass arrests, censorship, and the use of military force in civilian areas. While Trudeau framed these measures as necessary to protect national security and preserve law and order, many critics saw them as an overreach of power designed to stifle the political aspirations of Quebec nationalists and other dissenting voices.

The Context: Quebec Separatism and the FLQ

The October Crisis was the culmination of a decade-long rise in separatist sentiment in Quebec, where the desire for greater autonomy from Canada and, in some cases, outright independence, had grown significantly. This movement was fueled by a deep sense of cultural and economic marginalization within the broader Canadian federation, where Anglophone dominance in government and business had long sidelined Quebec's Francophone majority.

The FLQ, a small but militant group of Quebec separatists, emerged in the 1960s and began using violence to achieve its goals. The FLQ's tactics included bombings, robberies, and eventually, kidnappings. Their violent activities were not representative of the broader Quebec sovereignty movement, but they garnered widespread attention and created a climate of fear. The FLQ's ultimate goal was to overthrow the federal government's control of Quebec and establish an independent socialist state.

By October 1970, the FLQ had escalated its activities by kidnapping British diplomat James Cross and Quebec Minister of Labour Pierre Laporte. This act of terrorism shocked the nation and forced Prime Minister Pierre

Trudeau to respond. Faced with mounting pressure to restore order, Trudeau invoked the War Measures Act on October 16, 1970, a move that dramatically expanded the federal government's powers under the pretext of protecting national security.

The War Measures Act: A Tool for Silencing Dissent

The War Measures Act, originally passed during World War I, was designed to give the federal government extraordinary powers in times of war or national emergency. By invoking the Act during peacetime, Trudeau granted the government the ability to suspend civil liberties, including the right to habeas corpus (protection from arbitrary detention), freedom of movement, and freedom of assembly. These measures allowed the police and military to arrest individuals without charge and detain them indefinitely, while also restricting public gatherings and censoring the press.

While the government justified the use of the War Measures Act as necessary to prevent further acts of terrorism by the FLQ, its scope quickly expanded beyond combatting the militant group. Over 450 people were arrested during the crackdown, many of whom were not connected to the FLQ or its violent activities. Political activists, intellectuals, artists, and community leaders who supported Quebec sovereignty or were critical of the federal government's approach to the crisis were among those detained. The arrests included prominent Quebec nationalists who had publicly denounced violence but were nonetheless viewed as a threat by the federal government.

The mass detentions, which were carried out without due process, were widely seen as an attempt to silence political dissent under the guise of maintaining national security. Many of those arrested were vocal critics of the federal government's treatment of Quebec and its Francophone population. By detaining these individuals, the Trudeau government effectively stifled political opposition and sent a message to Quebec's separatist movement that dissent would not be tolerated.

Trudeau's Justification and the Ethics of Overreach

When questioned about his government's use of the War Measures Act and the suspension of civil liberties, Pierre Trudeau famously responded with the phrase, "Just watch me." This statement came to symbolize his defiant attitude toward critics who argued that the government was overstepping its authority. For Trudeau, the October Crisis represented an existential threat to Canada's unity and national security, and he believed that extraordinary measures were necessary to restore order and prevent further violence.

However, critics argued that Trudeau's heavy-handed response was disproportionate to the actual threat posed by the FLQ. While the FLQ had engaged in acts of terrorism, the group was relatively small, and its violent activities did not represent the broader Quebec separatist movement. By invoking the War Measures Act and using it to detain political dissidents, the Trudeau government blurred the line between combatting terrorism and suppressing legitimate political expression.

The ethical implications of this overreach were significant. While the government framed its actions as necessary to protect public safety, the mass arrests of individuals who had no connection to terrorism raised questions about the true motivations behind the crackdown. Many argued that Trudeau was using the FLQ crisis as a pretext to stifle political opposition in Quebec and to send a message to the broader sovereignty movement that dissent would not be tolerated. This use of state power to silence political opposition under the guise of national security has been a point of contention in Canadian politics ever since.

Broader Implications: Setting a Precedent for Government Overreach

The use of the War Measures Act during the October Crisis set a dangerous precedent for government overreach in times of crisis. By suspending civil liberties and granting itself extraordinary powers, the Trudeau government demonstrated how easily democratic rights can be curtailed when framed as necessary for national security. This raised concerns about how future governments might use similar tactics to suppress dissent or consolidate power during moments of political instability.

For Quebec nationalists and supporters of the sovereignty movement, the October Crisis reinforced the perception that Ottawa was willing to use force and repression to maintain control over the province. The mass arrests and military presence on the streets of Quebec further alienated many Quebecers, who viewed Trudeau's actions as an affront to their political rights and cultural identity. The crisis deepened the divide between Quebec and the rest of Canada, contributing to the rise of the Parti Québécois and leading to two referendums on Quebec independence in the following decades.

The October Crisis also had broader implications for how Canadians viewed the balance between security and civil liberties. While many Canadians initially supported Trudeau's decision to invoke the War Measures Act, believing that it was necessary to prevent further violence, there was growing discomfort in the years that followed over the extent of the government's crackdown. The arrests, military deployment, and the targeting of political dissidents created a chilling effect on political activism, particularly within the Quebec sovereignty movement. The message sent by the federal government was clear: dissent, especially when it questioned the unity of the Canadian state, would be met with force. This set a dangerous precedent for how far the government was willing to go to maintain control under the guise of national security.

For many, the October Crisis demonstrated how a government could exploit fear and uncertainty to consolidate power and suppress political opposition. While the FLQ's violent actions warranted a response, the invocation of the War Measures Act extended far beyond addressing the immediate threat posed by terrorism. The Trudeau government's decision to detain hundreds of political activists, intellectuals, and community leaders without charge signaled a broader intent to weaken the Quebec sovereignty movement as a whole, regardless of its connection to violence.

Targeting of Non-Violent Political Dissidents

One of the most troubling aspects of the government's response during the October Crisis was the targeting of non-violent political dissidents. Many of the 450 people arrested under the War Measures Act were not involved in the FLQ's terrorist activities, but were instead outspoken critics of the federal government's treatment of Quebec or advocates for Quebec sovereignty. These individuals included journalists, labor union leaders, intellectuals, and artists—people who had no direct ties to the FLQ but were nonetheless seen as a threat to federal authority.

This use of government power to silence political dissent was widely condemned as an abuse of state authority. Critics argued that the arrests were not about stopping terrorism, but rather about sending a message to Quebecers who supported greater autonomy or independence: that Ottawa would not tolerate any challenges to the unity of Canada. By conflating terrorism with political activism, the Trudeau government undermined the distinction between violent extremists and legitimate political actors, casting a wide net over anyone who questioned the status quo.

Among the most notable critics of the government's response was the civil liberties community. Human rights organizations and political commentators raised alarms about the long-term consequences of suspending civil liberties in response to a relatively isolated crisis. The arbitrary arrests and lack of due process violated the fundamental principles of justice, and many feared that the War Measures Act had set a dangerous precedent for future abuses of power by the federal government.

The Legacy of the War Measures Act and Trudeau's Centralization of Power

The October Crisis and the use of the War Measures Act have left a lasting legacy in Canadian politics. Pierre Trudeau's decision to invoke such extreme measures during a domestic crisis fundamentally altered the relationship between the federal government and its citizens, as well as between Ottawa and Quebec. The widespread use of military force and the suspension of civil liberties in response to the FLQ's actions left many Quebecers feeling alienated and resentful toward the federal government.

The political and cultural consequences of the October Crisis contributed to the rise of the Parti Québécois, which would go on to win the 1976 provincial election under the leadership of René Lévesque. The PQ's success was driven, in part, by the perception that Ottawa was unwilling to respect Quebec's desire for greater autonomy. The party's push for a referendum on Quebec's independence was a direct challenge to the centralized power that Trudeau had sought to consolidate during the crisis.

On a national level, the October Crisis raised critical questions about how governments should balance the need for security with the protection of civil liberties. While the FLQ's violent actions required a response, many Canadians came to view the invocation of the War Measures Act as an overreach that unnecessarily violated the rights of innocent citizens. The long-term impact of the October Crisis shaped debates around civil liberties, the role of the military in domestic affairs, and the limits of government power in times of crisis.

Trudeau's handling of the October Crisis also fits into a broader pattern of his leadership, characterized by a strong centralizing tendency. Throughout his time as Prime Minister, Trudeau sought to strengthen federal authority, often at the expense of provincial autonomy. The October Crisis was perhaps the most dramatic example of this centralization of power, as it demonstrated his willingness to use extraordinary measures to suppress political opposition in the name of national unity.

Pierre Trudeau's response to the October Crisis through the invocation of the War Measures Act stands as one of the most controversial moments in Canadian history.

While Trudeau justified his actions as necessary to prevent further violence and maintain national security, the scope of the government's response—mass arrests, military deployments, and the suspension of civil liberties—revealed a willingness to prioritize state control over individual freedoms.

The heavy-handed use of government power to silence political dissent under the guise of combatting terrorism was a critical turning point in Canada's national discourse on civil rights and security. The ethical implications of this decision continue to resonate today, as it raised fundamental questions about the limits of government authority in times of crisis. For many Quebecers and civil rights advocates, the October Crisis demonstrated how easily the machinery of government can be turned against its own citizens, particularly when political dissent challenges the status quo.

Ultimately, the October Crisis left an indelible mark on Canada's political landscape. It deepened the divide between Quebec and the rest of the country, fueled the rise of the sovereignty movement, and set a troubling precedent for the use of extraordinary state power to silence political opposition. While Pierre Trudeau's leadership during the crisis has been praised for its decisiveness, it also serves as a cautionary tale about the dangers of sacrificing civil liberties in the name of national security.

Part II: Justin Trudeau – Inheritor of a Corrupt Legacy

Chapter 5: The Rise of Justin Trudeau

Justin Trudeau's Rapid Political Ascent: Fueled by the Trudeau Name Rather Than Merit or Competency

Justin Trudeau's rise to power in Canadian politics was swift, and from the beginning, it was clear that his ascent was propelled more by his famous last name and the political legacy of his father, Pierre Elliott Trudeau, than by his own merit or demonstrated competency. While Trudeau presented himself as a fresh face in Canadian politics—young, energetic, and progressive—critics argue that his rapid rise was a product of political branding rather than a reflection of his personal qualifications or achievements.

As the son of one of Canada's most iconic and polarizing Prime Ministers, Justin Trudeau benefited immensely from the political capital that came with the Trudeau name. His familial connection to Pierre Trudeau imbued him with a certain level of credibility and recognition that few politicians could ever dream of, regardless of their qualifications. Despite a thin résumé, Trudeau was able to leverage his family's legacy to gain support from the Liberal Party, eventually becoming leader and winning the 2015 federal election. His rapid ascent to the highest office in the land was, for many, a clear example of political privilege trumping merit.

A Shallow Resume: From Drama Teacher to Prime Minister

Before entering politics, Justin Trudeau's professional background was not in governance, law, or business, but in education. He worked as a drama teacher and snowboard instructor, and briefly studied engineering and environmental geography—none of which suggested that he was particularly qualified to lead a major political party, let alone the country. In terms of policy experience, Trudeau had little to show when he first entered politics. His involvement in public life was largely limited to charity events and public speaking engagements, which were, again, bolstered by his father's legacy rather than his own contributions.

Trudeau's formal entrance into politics came in 2008, when he was elected as the Member of Parliament for the riding of Papineau in Montreal. Even then, his candidacy was seen by many as a product of his family's influence rather than any particular competency or skill on his part. While his campaign focused on broad themes of change and youth engagement, it lacked substantive policy proposals, relying heavily on the Trudeau brand to carry him to victory. His election was less about his qualifications and more about the electorate's nostalgia for his father and a desire for political dynasties to continue.

The Trudeau Brand: A Legacy Leveraged for Power

From the moment he entered the public eye, Justin Trudeau made little effort to distance himself from his father's legacy. In fact, he leaned into it, using the Trudeau name as a powerful political brand that resonated with a generation of Canadians who had grown up during Pierre Trudeau's time in office. The name carried a sense of nostalgia, particularly among Liberal Party supporters, who viewed Pierre Trudeau as a champion of progressive values, national unity, and a defender of civil rights. For many, supporting Justin Trudeau was akin to keeping the Trudeau legacy alive.

However, this reliance on his father's political legacy raised significant concerns about Justin's own competency. Critics argued that he lacked the depth of experience and understanding needed to govern effectively, and that his reliance on his family's name was a sign that he was not prepared to tackle the complexities of leading a country. Trudeau's political speeches and platforms often echoed the same themes his father had championed—national unity, multiculturalism, and progressive social policies—but they lacked the intellectual rigor and depth that had characterized Pierre Trudeau's policies.

Despite this, the Trudeau name remained a powerful asset, and it played a key role in Justin's ascension to the leadership of the Liberal Party in 2013. His leadership campaign was built around the idea that he could reinvigorate the party and the country by drawing on his father's legacy, even though his qualifications and experience paled in comparison to other political leaders of his generation. The overwhelming support he received within the Liberal Party was largely a reflection of the power of political branding, rather than a recognition of his capabilities as a leader.

Style Over Substance: Trudeau's Political Appeal

One of the key elements of Justin Trudeau's political ascent was his ability to appeal to voters through his charisma and charm, even if this came at the expense of substantive policy discussions. Trudeau's political style was heavily based on imagery and rhetoric—projecting youth, vitality, and progressivism while offering little in terms of concrete policies or governance strategies. His 2015 election campaign, for example, focused heavily on themes of "real change" and "sunny ways," but critics pointed out that these slogans were often devoid of detailed plans for addressing the pressing issues facing Canada.

The media played a significant role in bolstering Trudeau's image as a fresh, dynamic leader, often ignoring his lack of experience and focusing instead on his personal charisma and his family's legacy. His good looks, charm, and ability to connect with young voters on platforms like social media helped him craft an image of a modern, forward-thinking politician, even if that image was not always backed by substance. In many ways, Trudeau's rise to power can be seen as a triumph of style over substance—an appeal to voters' emotions and desire for change rather than a reflection of his competency to govern.

His campaign capitalized on this image-driven approach, positioning him as a contrast to the more conservative, and arguably more experienced, Stephen Harper. Trudeau's promises to legalize marijuana, champion environmental causes, and support Indigenous rights resonated with a wide swath of the electorate, even though his specific policy proposals in these areas were often vague or incomplete. His rise to power was characterized by broad, feel-good rhetoric that appealed to voters' desire for optimism, rather than a substantive track record of leadership or policy expertise.

Lack of Competency and Scandals in Office

Once in power, Trudeau's lack of political experience and depth became more evident, as his government faced numerous challenges that highlighted his inability to effectively manage key aspects of governance. Early in his tenure, Trudeau was criticized for his handling of several major issues, including foreign policy, fiscal management, and ethical scandals. His approach to these challenges often appeared disconnected, highlighting his inexperience and the limits of his political skill.

One of the most glaring examples of Trudeau's lack of competency came in the form of the SNC-Lavalin scandal. In 2019, Trudeau's government was rocked by allegations that he had interfered in the criminal prosecution of a Quebec-based construction company,

SNC-Lavalin, to protect jobs in Quebec. The scandal, which involved allegations of political favoritism and corruption, led to the resignation of several key cabinet members, including his Attorney General, Jody Wilson-Raybould. The incident not only revealed Trudeau's susceptibility to ethical lapses but also reinforced the perception that his rapid rise to power was not supported by the political acumen needed to effectively govern.

The WE Charity scandal in 2020 further underscored Trudeau's questionable judgment and lack of leadership competency. His government was accused of awarding a lucrative contract to a charity with close ties to the Trudeau family, raising serious concerns about conflicts of interest. The scandal, along with Trudeau's repeated ethical lapses, demonstrated that his political ascent had not been accompanied by the leadership skills required

Justin Trudeau's political career is a clear example of how a famous last name and an iconic political legacy can propel someone to power, even in the absence of merit or competency. His rapid rise to the position of Prime Minister was fueled by the Trudeau brand, nostalgia for his father's leadership, and a carefully crafted image of youthful optimism and progressivism. However, once in power, Trudeau's lack of political experience and depth of understanding became apparent, as his government struggled with ethical scandals, policy mismanagement, and questions about his leadership abilities.

Trudeau's ascent may have been rapid, but it was not built on a foundation of demonstrated competency. Instead, it was driven by the power of political branding and the public's willingness to invest in an image of leadership, rather than the reality. While Trudeau remains a polarizing figure, his rise to power offers a cautionary tale about the dangers of elevating leaders based on legacy and charisma, rather than merit and ability.

Media Manipulation and the Creation of a Celebrity-Style Leader with Little Substance: The Justin Trudeau Phenomenon

Justin Trudeau's rise to power in Canadian politics is as much a media creation as it is a result of his political strategy. From the early days of his public life, the media played a crucial role in shaping his image, presenting him not as a seasoned politician but as a youthful, charismatic figure who embodied change and progress. However, as his time in office has revealed, Trudeau's political success has often relied on media manipulation and the crafting of a celebrity-style persona, with little substantive policy or leadership behind the image. This reliance on superficial charm and carefully controlled public relations strategies has led critics to argue that Trudeau represents the triumph of style over substance in modern politics.

Trudeau's ability to dominate the political landscape, particularly in the early years of his leadership, can be attributed in large part to the media's role in promoting his image while downplaying or ignoring his lack of political experience and depth. The creation of this celebrity-style leader allowed Trudeau to connect emotionally with voters and craft an appealing narrative of youthful idealism and progressive values. However, this media-driven portrayal often obscured his shallow policy proposals and inability to deliver on many of his promises.

The Media's Role in Shaping the Trudeau Image

From the outset, Trudeau's media image was one of his greatest political assets. As the son of Pierre Trudeau, one of Canada's most iconic prime ministers, Justin was already a familiar name, and the media capitalized on this legacy by framing him as the natural heir to his father's progressive vision. While Justin had relatively little political experience when he entered public life, the media quickly latched onto his charisma, good looks, and youth, crafting a narrative of him as a fresh face who could reinvigorate the Liberal Party and lead the country into a new era of progressive change.

This narrative was often built on superficial qualities rather than substantive policy achievements. Trudeau's candidacy was treated by many media outlets like the rise of a pop culture figure rather than a serious political leader. Media reports focused on his family name, his personal charm, and his ability to attract large crowds, while offering little in the way of critical analysis of his policy positions or his qualifications for office. The focus on his celebrity-style appeal meant that Trudeau's flaws, including his lack of experience and depth, were often glossed over or ignored.

One key example of this media manipulation came during Trudeau's bid for leadership of the Liberal Party in 2013. While his opponents had years of experience and a deeper understanding of policy, Trudeau's candidacy was buoyed by media coverage that portrayed him as the inevitable choice for leader due to his ability to "connect" with voters. This coverage focused more on his personal appeal than on his ability to govern, laying the groundwork for his eventual rise to the office of Prime Minister in 2015.

The Celebrity-Style Leader: Image Over Substance

Trudeau's tenure as Prime Minister has been marked by a continued reliance on media-driven narratives that emphasize his image as a celebrity-style leader, often at the expense of substantive policy discussions. This style of leadership was particularly evident in the early years of his government, when Trudeau was frequently seen engaging in high-profile public relations stunts that were designed to boost his personal brand rather than address pressing policy issues.

Trudeau's use of social media, in particular, was a key element in building his celebrity-style leadership. His carefully curated Instagram account, filled with images of him taking selfies, engaging with young voters, and participating in feel-good events, helped cement his image as a modern, relatable leader who was in touch with ordinary Canadians. However, this focus on style and presentation often masked a lack of depth in his policy positions. While Trudeau spoke eloquently about progressive values such as feminism, Indigenous rights, and climate change, his government's actual policies in these areas were often criticized as lacking in meaningful action or substance.

The reliance on media appearances and social media to craft his image has also led to criticism that Trudeau's leadership is more about optics than governance. His frequent appearances at high-profile events, such as international summits or celebrity-filled galas, often created the impression that Trudeau was more interested in maintaining his public image than in addressing the real challenges facing Canadians. For example, his much-publicized state visit to India in 2018, during which he donned traditional Indian clothing and posed for photographs with Bollywood celebrities, was widely criticized as a media stunt that overshadowed the actual diplomatic purpose of the trip. This event, among others, highlighted the disconnect between Trudeau's image as a global leader and his ability to engage in serious policy discussions.

Media Bias and Lack of Scrutiny

One of the key factors in Trudeau's ability to maintain his celebrity-style leadership has been the media's often unquestioning support of his image, particularly during his early years as Prime Minister. While political leaders typically face scrutiny from the press, Trudeau benefited from a media environment that was largely sympathetic to his progressive messaging and focused more on his personal appeal than on his policy failures.

Trudeau's ability to control his media image was further bolstered by the Liberal government's decision to provide significant funding to struggling Canadian media outlets. In 2018, Trudeau's government announced a nearly $600 million media bailout package aimed at supporting journalism in Canada. While this funding was framed as a necessary measure to support the free press, critics argued that it created an environment in which media outlets were less likely to criticize the government, fearing the loss of financial support.

This perceived conflict of interest raised questions about the independence of the Canadian media and whether Trudeau was manipulating the media landscape to maintain favorable coverage. Critics pointed out that many major media outlets, which benefited from government funding, were reluctant to engage in critical analysis of Trudeau's leadership, particularly when it came to scandals such as the SNC-Lavalin affair or the WE Charity controversy. The result was a media environment in which Trudeau's flaws were downplayed or ignored, allowing his celebrity-style image to persist despite mounting evidence of his government's ethical lapses and policy failures.

The Consequences of a Shallow Leader

The creation of a celebrity-style leader with little substance has had significant consequences for Canadian politics and governance. While Trudeau's media-savvy approach allowed him to connect with voters and win elections, it also led to a government that struggled to deliver on many of its promises. Trudeau's frequent reliance on feel-good messaging and image-driven leadership has led to a disconnect between the lofty ideals he espouses and the concrete policies he has been able to implement.

One of the most glaring examples of this disconnect is Trudeau's approach to climate change. While he has positioned himself as a global leader on environmental issues, his government has faced criticism for approving major oil pipeline projects and failing to meet Canada's emissions reduction targets. Similarly, his government's handling of Indigenous issues has been criticized for failing to deliver on key promises, such as clean drinking water for First Nations communities and meaningful reconciliation efforts.

The reliance on media manipulation and image-driven leadership has also eroded trust in Trudeau's government. As scandals such as the SNC-Lavalin affair and the WE Charity controversy have come to light, it has become increasingly clear that Trudeau's celebrity-style image does not align with the ethical and policy failures of his government. This dissonance has led to growing disillusionment among voters, many of whom were initially drawn to Trudeau's promise of real change but have since become frustrated by his government's lack of substance

Chapter 6: Ethics Violations and Scandals

The SNC-Lavalin Scandal

The SNC-Lavalin Affair: Justin Trudeau's Attempt to Interfere in a Criminal Prosecution to Benefit a Quebec-Based Corporation

The SNC-Lavalin affair, one of the most significant scandals of Justin Trudeau's time as Prime Minister, exposed serious ethical concerns about the integrity of his leadership and his commitment to the rule of law. The scandal centered around allegations that Trudeau and senior members of his government attempted to interfere in a criminal prosecution involving SNC-Lavalin, a large Quebec-based engineering and construction firm. The affair raised questions about political favoritism, government overreach, and Trudeau's willingness to protect powerful corporate interests at the expense of Canada's legal institutions.

The SNC-Lavalin affair highlighted Trudeau's ties to Quebec, where SNC-Lavalin is a major employer, and cast a shadow over his image as a progressive leader dedicated to transparency, justice, and fairness. The scandal led to high-profile resignations within his cabinet, damaged his credibility, and eroded public trust in his government.

Background: SNC-Lavalin's Legal Troubles

SNC-Lavalin is a multinational engineering firm headquartered in Montreal, Quebec, with a long history of involvement in major infrastructure projects across Canada and around the world. However, the company's reputation was tarnished by allegations of corruption and bribery, particularly in connection with its operations in Libya during the regime of Muammar Gaddafi. Between 2001 and 2011, SNC-Lavalin allegedly paid millions of dollars in bribes to Libyan officials to secure lucrative construction contracts. These activities were part of a broader pattern of corruption within the company that led to investigations by Canadian authorities.

In 2015, the Royal Canadian Mounted Police (RCMP) charged SNC-Lavalin with fraud and corruption related to its dealings in Libya. If convicted, the company faced severe penalties, including being barred from bidding on federal contracts for 10 years. This potential ban posed a significant threat to the company's business and its ability to operate in Canada, where federal contracts were a substantial part of its revenue stream.

Trudeau's Attempt to Interfere: The Deferred Prosecution Agreement

In 2018, Justin Trudeau's government introduced legislation allowing for the use of deferred prosecution agreements (DPAs), a legal mechanism that allows companies accused of wrongdoing to avoid criminal prosecution in exchange for admitting guilt, paying fines, and agreeing to corrective measures. DPAs are often used to avoid the economic fallout that can result from criminal convictions, particularly when large corporations are involved.

SNC-Lavalin sought to take advantage of this new legal tool by negotiating a DPA with the federal government, which would allow it to avoid criminal prosecution and continue bidding on government contracts. However, the Public Prosecution Service of Canada (PPSC), an independent federal agency responsible for overseeing criminal prosecutions, declined to offer SNC-Lavalin a DPA. The PPSC determined that the charges against the company were too serious to be resolved through a deferred prosecution agreement and that SNC-Lavalin should face a full trial.

At this point, Trudeau and his inner circle allegedly became involved. According to testimonies and reports that emerged during the scandal, Trudeau and senior officials from the Prime Minister's Office (PMO) pressured then-Attorney General and Minister of Justice Jody Wilson-Raybould to overrule the PPSC's decision and instruct prosecutors to negotiate a DPA with SNC-Lavalin. Wilson-Raybould, however, resisted this pressure, asserting that it would be inappropriate for her to interfere in the independent decision-making process of the prosecutors.

The pressure allegedly continued for months, with Trudeau and his senior aides engaging in repeated conversations with Wilson-Raybould about the SNC-Lavalin case. According to Wilson-Raybould, she was told that a criminal trial could result in significant job losses in Quebec, where SNC-Lavalin employed thousands of workers. Trudeau and his team framed the issue as a matter of protecting jobs, but critics argued that the government was more concerned with protecting a politically connected corporation based in Quebec, a key electoral battleground for the Liberal Party.

Jody Wilson-Raybould's Resignation and Whistleblowing

Jody Wilson-Raybould's refusal to intervene on behalf of SNC-Lavalin ultimately led to her demotion in January 2019, when Trudeau reassigned her to the position of Minister of Veterans Affairs. Many observers viewed this move as retaliation for her refusal to comply with the Prime Minister's wishes. In February 2019, Wilson-Raybould resigned from the cabinet, setting off a political firestorm.

Following her resignation, Wilson-Raybould testified before the House of Commons Justice Committee, revealing the extent of the pressure she faced from Trudeau and senior government officials to intervene in the SNC-Lavalin case. In her testimony, she described what she called a "consistent and sustained effort" by the Prime Minister's Office to influence her decision, despite her repeated insistence that it was inappropriate for the government to interfere in a criminal prosecution.

Wilson-Raybould's testimony was a bombshell, providing detailed accounts of meetings and conversations in which Trudeau's aides allegedly pressured her to find a solution that would allow SNC-Lavalin to avoid criminal prosecution. She also revealed that Trudeau himself had raised concerns about the potential political fallout of a trial, particularly in

Quebec, where job losses could hurt the Liberal Party's electoral prospects.

The revelations led to widespread public outrage and raised serious questions about Trudeau's commitment to upholding the rule of law and maintaining the independence of Canada's judicial system. The scandal damaged Trudeau's reputation as a progressive leader dedicated to transparency and fairness and cast doubt on his ability to separate political interests from legal decision-making.

The Aftermath: Resignations and Political Fallout

The SNC-Lavalin affair triggered a series of high-profile resignations within Trudeau's government. In addition to Wilson-Raybould, Jane Philpott, another senior Liberal cabinet minister, resigned in solidarity, citing concerns about the government's handling of the affair and its broader ethical implications. Trudeau's principal secretary, Gerald Butts, also resigned, though he denied any wrongdoing.

The scandal also led to a sharp decline in Trudeau's approval ratings and created deep divisions within the Liberal Party. While some members of the party defended Trudeau's actions, arguing that he was trying to protect Canadian jobs, others expressed concern about the damage the affair had done to the party's reputation and its commitment to ethical governance.

In August 2019, Canada's Ethics Commissioner released a report on the SNC-Lavalin affair, concluding that Trudeau had violated the Conflict of Interest Act by improperly pressuring Wilson-Raybould to intervene in the prosecution. The report found that Trudeau had used his position of authority to advance the private interests of SNC-Lavalin and had undermined the independence of the Attorney General's office. The Ethics Commissioner's findings further damaged Trudeau's credibility, particularly as the scandal broke in the lead-up to the 2019 federal election.

The SNC-Lavalin affair was a defining scandal of Justin Trudeau's tenure as Prime Minister, revealing the lengths to which he and his government were willing to go to protect a powerful Quebec-based corporation. The scandal exposed serious ethical lapses within Trudeau's administration, including attempts to interfere in the independent judicial process and political favoritism toward a company with close ties to the Liberal Party.

Trudeau's handling of the SNC-Lavalin affair damaged his reputation as a progressive leader committed to transparency, ethics, and the rule of law. The revelations of political interference and the subsequent fallout raised questions about his ability to navigate the balance between economic interests and the independence of Canada's legal institutions. Ultimately, the affair remains a black mark on Trudeau's legacy and continues to serve as a cautionary tale about the dangers of political favoritism and government overreach.

Connections Between the Trudeau Government and Corporate Elites

One of the most persistent criticisms of Justin Trudeau's leadership has been the close relationship between his government and corporate elites. Despite positioning himself as a progressive champion for the middle class, Trudeau's administration has been repeatedly accused of favoring powerful business interests over ordinary Canadians. These accusations have been bolstered by scandals like the SNC-Lavalin affair, the WE Charity controversy, and policies that critics argue prioritize corporate interests over public welfare.

Trudeau's relationship with corporate elites raises questions about the extent to which corporate influence has shaped government decision-making under his leadership. Whether through political favoritism, backdoor dealings, or the use of government power to protect the interests of large corporations, the Trudeau government has been accused of reinforcing the power of Canada's corporate class while maintaining a public image of progressive governance.

The SNC-Lavalin Affair: Corporate Influence in Action

The SNC-Lavalin affair is perhaps the clearest example of the Trudeau government's close ties to corporate elites. SNC-Lavalin, one of Canada's largest engineering and construction firms, faced criminal charges for bribery and corruption related to its business dealings in

Libya. In 2018, the Trudeau government introduced legislation that allowed for deferred prosecution agreements (DPAs), a legal mechanism that allows corporations to avoid criminal prosecution in exchange for fines and remedial measures. This move appeared tailor-made to benefit SNC-Lavalin, which was seeking to avoid a criminal trial and the potential for being banned from bidding on federal contracts.

The subsequent pressure exerted by Trudeau and his senior staff on then-Attorney General Jody Wilson-Raybould to secure a DPA for SNC-Lavalin demonstrated how deeply the Trudeau government was willing to intervene to protect the interests of a powerful corporation. The argument put forth by Trudeau's team was that a criminal trial could lead to significant job losses in Quebec, where SNC-Lavalin is headquartered. However, critics pointed out that the pressure to intervene in the legal process seemed more aligned with protecting a well-connected corporate ally than with safeguarding jobs.

Wilson-Raybould's refusal to comply with the demands to secure a DPA led to her demotion and subsequent resignation, resulting in a political firestorm. The scandal underscored the extent to which Trudeau was willing to go to protect SNC-Lavalin, revealing the government's close relationship with a major corporate player. The Ethics Commissioner's report later concluded that Trudeau had violated the Conflict of Interest Act by attempting to influence the Attorney General, further highlighting the ethical issues surrounding the government's ties to corporate elites.

The WE Charity Scandal: Government Contracts and Corporate Ties

Another example of the Trudeau government's connections to corporate elites emerged in the form of the WE Charity scandal in 2020. The Trudeau government awarded a $912 million contract to the WE Charity to administer a student volunteer program during the COVID-19 pandemic. The decision sparked controversy when it was revealed that members of the Trudeau family, including the Prime Minister's wife, mother, and brother, had been paid hundreds of thousands of dollars for speaking engagements at WE Charity events.

The scandal raised serious questions about conflicts of interest and the government's decision-making process. Critics argued that the Trudeau government was using public funds to benefit a charity with close personal ties to the Prime Minister's family. While Trudeau denied any wrongdoing and claimed that the WE Charity was chosen for its ability to manage the program, the perception of favoritism and cronyism damaged the government's credibility.

The Ethics Commissioner launched an investigation into the matter, which ultimately highlighted how corporate connections and personal relationships within the Trudeau government had the potential to influence public policy and the allocation of government contracts. The WE Charity scandal served as yet another example of the government's apparent willingness to reward well-connected organizations with lucrative contracts, reinforcing the notion that corporate elites had privileged access to government resources under Trudeau's leadership.

Corporate Elites and Government Policy: The Energy Sector

The Trudeau government's policies on energy and the environment have also drawn criticism for being overly accommodating to corporate interests, particularly in the oil and gas sector. Despite positioning himself as a global leader in the fight against climate change, Trudeau's government has approved major oil pipeline projects, including the expansion of the Trans Mountain pipeline. These decisions have angered environmentalists and Indigenous groups, who argue that the government is prioritizing the interests of large energy companies over the health of the environment and the rights of Indigenous peoples.

Trudeau's support for the oil and gas industry has been framed by his government as necessary to maintain economic stability and protect jobs. However, critics argue that these policies reflect the government's close ties to corporate elites in the energy sector, who have historically wielded significant influence in Canadian politics. The approval of the Trans Mountain pipeline, in particular, demonstrated the government's willingness to balance environmental rhetoric with actions that support powerful corporate interests.

Moreover, the Canadian Association of Petroleum Producers (CAPP), one of the most powerful industry groups in the country, has had considerable access to Trudeau's government. Reports have shown that CAPP lobbyists met with government officials hundreds of times during Trudeau's tenure, raising concerns about the extent to which corporate elites in the energy sector are shaping public policy. This has led to accusations that Trudeau's government is more concerned with protecting corporate profits than with meaningfully addressing climate change.

Government Bailouts and Corporate Interests

During the COVID-19 pandemic, the Trudeau government introduced a series of economic relief measures designed to support Canadian businesses and workers. While many of these programs were aimed at providing much-needed assistance to small businesses and individuals, there were also significant bailouts directed toward large corporations, further fueling allegations of favoritism toward corporate elites.

One of the most controversial bailouts involved the airline industry, which received billions of dollars in government support. While airlines were struggling due to travel restrictions and the economic impact of the pandemic, critics argued that the government was too quick to funnel public money into large corporations without imposing sufficient conditions, such as protecting workers or limiting executive bonuses. The airline bailout was seen by many as yet another example of the Trudeau government's tendency to prioritize corporate elites during times of crisis.

In addition to the airline industry, the Trudeau government's relief measures included substantial support for the oil and gas sector, which faced significant challenges due to falling global demand and plummeting oil prices. The federal government provided billions in loans and subsidies to energy companies, leading environmentalists and progressive groups to accuse Trudeau of using the pandemic as an excuse to prop up fossil fuel industries rather than investing in renewable energy and a green economic recovery.

The Influence of Corporate Lobbying

Corporate lobbying has been a persistent issue throughout Justin Trudeau's tenure, with corporate elites maintaining significant access to government officials and decision-makers. Lobbying records reveal that major corporations, industry groups, and their representatives have been highly active in influencing the government's policies on everything from energy and infrastructure to telecommunications and finance.

For example, SNC-Lavalin, which played a central role in the 2019 corruption scandal, has continued to lobby the government on various issues related to infrastructure projects and government contracts.

Similarly, corporations in the pharmaceutical, tech, and banking sectors have maintained strong relationships with Trudeau's government, meeting regularly with key officials to shape policy decisions in ways that benefit their industries.

While lobbying is a legal and common part of the political process, the close ties between corporate elites and the Trudeau government raise concerns about the extent to which public policy is being shaped by corporate interests rather than by the needs of ordinary Canadians. The repeated instances of scandals and controversial policies involving corporate players have led to a growing perception that Trudeau's government is more concerned with appeasing powerful business interests than with serving the public good.

The Trudeau government's ties to corporate elites have been a recurring theme throughout Justin Trudeau's tenure as Prime Minister. From the SNC-Lavalin affair to the WE Charity scandal, and from pipeline approvals to corporate bailouts during the COVID-19 pandemic, Trudeau has repeatedly faced accusations of prioritizing corporate interests over the public good. While his government has framed many of these actions as necessary to protect jobs and maintain economic stability, critics argue that the influence of corporate elites has distorted public policy and undermined trust in the government's commitment to transparency and fairness.

The repeated controversies surrounding corporate favoritism have damaged Trudeau's image as a progressive leader and raised serious ethical questions about the extent to which powerful corporations have shaped decision-making within his administration. As Trudeau continues to navigate the challenges of governing, the perception of corporate influence will remain a critical issue for his government and for the broader public discourse on the balance of power in Canadian politics.

- **WE Charity Scandal**

Examining the WE Charity Controversy: How the Trudeau Family Financially Benefited from a Government Contract Awarded Without Proper Due Process

The WE Charity controversy represents one of the most significant ethical scandals to occur during Justin Trudeau's tenure as Prime Minister of Canada. The scandal centers on the Trudeau government's decision to award a nearly $912 million federal contract to WE Charity to administer the Canada Student Service Grant (CSSG), a program designed to provide students with financial compensation for volunteer work during the COVID-19 pandemic. This decision raised significant concerns about conflicts of interest, as it was later revealed that members of the Trudeau family had been financially compensated by WE Charity for speaking engagements prior to the awarding of the contract.

The controversy highlighted deeper issues within the Trudeau government's handling of public funds, questions about favoritism, and the lack of transparency and due process in awarding lucrative government contracts. Trudeau's close personal ties to the organization and the financial benefits received by his family sparked widespread outrage, ultimately leading to multiple investigations and damaging his government's credibility.

Background: The Canada Student Service Grant (CSSG) and WE Charity

In response to the economic impact of the COVID-19 pandemic, the Trudeau government introduced a series of programs to support Canadians, including the Canada Student Service Grant (CSSG). The program aimed to help students whose summer employment prospects were affected by the pandemic by offering them up to $5,000 in grants in exchange for volunteer work. However, rather than allowing the federal government to manage the program, the Trudeau government outsourced the administration of the CSSG to WE Charity, an organization that focuses on youth empowerment and global social justice initiatives.

The decision to award the contract to WE Charity immediately raised concerns, as the organization had never managed a program of such scale. Furthermore, the contract was awarded without a competitive bidding process, leading to questions about why WE Charity had been chosen over other organizations or government agencies that may have been more qualified to administer the program.

Financial Ties Between the Trudeau Family and WE Charity

As scrutiny of the government's decision grew, it was revealed that members of Justin Trudeau's immediate family had received significant financial compensation from WE Charity for participating in various speaking engagements and events. These payments raised serious concerns about conflicts of interest, as Trudeau himself had not recused himself from the discussions surrounding the awarding of the contract to WE Charity.

The financial connections between the Trudeau family and WE Charity were as follows:

- **Margaret Trudeau**, the Prime Minister's mother, received approximately $250,000 for speaking at multiple WE Charity events between 2016 and 2020.
- **Sacha Trudeau**, the Prime Minister's brother, received around $32,000 for his involvement with WE Charity.
- **Sophie Grégoire Trudeau**, the Prime Minister's wife, had also participated in WE Charity events

and hosted the organization's podcast, though she was not paid for this work.

While Trudeau maintained that these speaking engagements were unrelated to the government's decision to award the contract to WE Charity, the optics of the situation were damaging. The revelation that members of Trudeau's family had financially benefited from the organization called into question whether the decision to award the contract had been made impartially or if it had been influenced by Trudeau's personal connections.

Lack of Due Process in Awarding the Contract

One of the key issues in the WE Charity controversy was the lack of proper due process in awarding the nearly $1 billion contract to administer the CSSG program. The contract was awarded without a competitive bidding process, which typically ensures transparency, fairness, and that taxpayer money is being used efficiently. By bypassing this process, the Trudeau government opened itself up to allegations of favoritism and cronyism.

Further complicating the situation, it was later revealed that WE Charity had close ties not only to the Trudeau family but also to senior members of the government, including Finance Minister Bill Morneau. Morneau, like Trudeau, had close family ties to WE Charity, with his daughter working for the organization. Morneau had also traveled with WE Charity on trips to Kenya and

Ecuador, expenses for which he had failed to repay until after the controversy became public.

The lack of transparency and proper due process in awarding the contract led to calls for further investigation. Critics argued that the government's decision-making process was tainted by personal connections and that awarding such a large contract to an organization with financial ties to the Prime Minister's family was both unethical and improper.

Investigations and Political Fallout

In the wake of the controversy, multiple investigations were launched to determine whether the Trudeau government had violated ethical guidelines and whether conflicts of interest had influenced the awarding of the CSSG contract. The federal Ethics Commissioner, Mario Dion, began an investigation into whether Trudeau had breached the Conflict of Interest Act, marking the third such investigation into Trudeau's conduct during his time as Prime Minister.

During testimony before the House of Commons Finance Committee, Trudeau admitted that he had not recused himself from the discussions surrounding the WE Charity contract, despite his family's financial ties to the organization. However, he denied that there had been any wrongdoing, arguing that the decision to award the contract to WE Charity was based on the organization's ability to administer the program and not on personal connections.

Despite Trudeau's defense, the scandal had a significant impact on his government's credibility. The controversy led to the resignation of Finance Minister Bill Morneau, who admitted to failing to properly disclose his ties to WE Charity and to repaying the expenses for his trips to Kenya and Ecuador only after the scandal came to light. Morneau's resignation further fueled allegations of improper conduct within the Trudeau government and added to the growing perception that corporate and personal interests were influencing decision-making at the highest levels.

Damage to Trudeau's Credibility and Public Trust

The WE Charity controversy had far-reaching political consequences, severely damaging Trudeau's credibility and the public's trust in his government. The scandal undermined Trudeau's carefully crafted image as a progressive leader committed to transparency and fairness. It also called into question the government's handling of public funds during the COVID-19 pandemic, with many Canadians wondering whether other decisions had been influenced by personal or corporate interests.

The controversy also exacerbated broader concerns about Trudeau's ethics, following earlier scandals such as the SNC-Lavalin affair, in which the Prime Minister had been found to have violated the Conflict of Interest Act. The repeated ethical lapses led to growing frustration among both Trudeau's political opponents and the public, with many questioning whether Trudeau could be trusted to govern in the best interests of Canadians.

Although the government ultimately canceled the contract with WE Charity following the public outcry, the damage had already been done. The scandal, combined with the COVID-19 pandemic, contributed to a turbulent political climate that further eroded the public's confidence in the Trudeau government's ability to manage the country's affairs.

The WE Charity controversy serves as a key example of how personal and corporate interests can influence government decision-making, eroding public trust in democratic institutions. By awarding a nearly $1 billion contract to an organization with close financial ties to his family, Justin Trudeau opened himself up to accusations of favoritism, cronyism, and ethical misconduct. The lack of proper due process in awarding the contract, combined with the revelations of financial connections between the Trudeau family and WE Charity, raised serious concerns about the integrity of the government's actions.

The scandal not only damaged Trudeau's personal credibility but also highlighted broader issues within his administration, particularly the recurring pattern of ethical lapses and conflicts of interest. As investigations into the WE Charity controversy continue to unfold, the affair remains a black mark on Trudeau's legacy, further complicating his image as a leader committed to transparency, fairness, and public service.

Patterns of Favoritism and Conflicts of Interest Within Justin Trudeau's Government

Since taking office in 2015, Justin Trudeau's government has faced repeated allegations of favoritism and conflicts of interest, raising concerns about the ethical standards of the administration. These controversies have often centered around decisions that appeared to benefit political allies, corporate elites, or members of Trudeau's own family, prompting questions about whether the Prime Minister and his inner circle have consistently placed personal or political interests above the public good.

From the SNC-Lavalin affair to the WE Charity scandal, and a pattern of questionable appointments and decisions benefiting those with close ties to the government, Trudeau's administration has been marred by repeated accusations of unethical behavior. This pattern suggests a systemic problem within the government's decision-making processes, where personal connections and political expediency often take precedence over transparency, accountability, and the rule of law.

The SNC-Lavalin Affair: Corporate Favoritism and Political Interference

One of the most well-known examples of favoritism and conflicts of interest in Trudeau's government is the **SNC-Lavalin affair**, which erupted in 2019. As discussed earlier, the Prime Minister and senior members of his office were accused of pressuring then-Attorney General Jody Wilson-Raybould to intervene in a criminal prosecution against SNC-Lavalin, a Quebec-based engineering firm facing charges of corruption and bribery.

The affair illustrated how Trudeau's government appeared to prioritize the interests of a politically connected corporation over the rule of law. SNC-Lavalin, which employed thousands of people in Quebec, was a major player in Canadian business and had deep ties to the Liberal Party. The pressure exerted on Wilson-Raybould to secure a deferred prosecution agreement (DPA) for the company, allowing it to avoid a criminal trial, was widely seen as an attempt to shield SNC-Lavalin from the consequences of its illegal actions.

Critics argued that this intervention was driven by political favoritism, aimed at protecting jobs in Quebec ahead of a federal election and maintaining support for the Liberal Party in the province. The Ethics Commissioner's report on the matter confirmed that Trudeau had violated the Conflict of Interest Act by attempting to influence the independent decision of the Attorney General, further undermining the integrity of his government.

The WE Charity Scandal: Nepotism and Family Ties

The **WE Charity scandal** was another major controversy that highlighted patterns of favoritism and conflicts of interest within the Trudeau government. In this case, the government awarded a nearly $912 million contract to WE Charity to administer the Canada Student Service Grant (CSSG) without proper due process or a competitive bidding process. The charity had close ties to Trudeau and his family, with his mother, brother, and wife having received payments for speaking engagements at WE Charity events.

The financial connections between the Trudeau family and WE Charity raised serious ethical concerns about whether Trudeau had used his influence to steer the contract toward an organization with which he had personal ties. Although Trudeau denied any wrongdoing and argued that WE Charity was chosen because of its experience with youth programs, the optics of the situation and the lack of transparency in awarding the contract further damaged the public's trust in the government.

Additionally, former Finance Minister Bill Morneau, who also had close family ties to WE Charity, admitted to having accepted expenses-paid trips from the organization that he had failed to repay until the scandal became public. Morneau's resignation amid the fallout from the scandal underscored how deeply conflicts of interest had permeated the highest levels of Trudeau's government.

Political Appointments and Insider Favoritism

In addition to major scandals like SNC-Lavalin and WE Charity, Trudeau's government has also been criticized for a pattern of questionable political appointments that appear to benefit political insiders or those with close ties to the Liberal Party.

One notable example was the appointment of **Julie Payette** as Governor General of Canada. Payette, a former astronaut, was appointed by Trudeau in 2017, despite concerns about her past behavior in professional environments. In January 2021, she resigned from the position following an investigation into allegations of workplace harassment and a toxic environment under her leadership. Critics pointed out that Trudeau's government had not conducted a thorough vetting process before appointing her to the role, raising questions about the government's decision-making and favoritism in high-level appointments.

Another example of insider favoritism came when Trudeau's government was accused of appointing individuals with close ties to the Liberal Party to influential positions in government agencies and boards. These appointments were criticized for lacking transparency and for giving undue influence to individuals with political connections, rather than those with the necessary qualifications and expertise for the roles.

Corporate Lobbying and Preferential Access

The close relationship between Trudeau's government and corporate elites has also led to concerns about corporate lobbying and preferential access to decision-makers. Lobbying records have shown that powerful corporations and industry groups, such as SNC-Lavalin, the Canadian Association of Petroleum Producers (CAPP), and other major corporate players, have enjoyed extensive access to Trudeau's government, raising questions about the influence of corporate interests on public policy.

In the energy sector, for example, Trudeau's government faced criticism for approving major oil pipeline projects, such as the Trans Mountain pipeline expansion, despite environmental concerns and opposition from Indigenous communities. Critics argued that the decision to approve these projects reflected the government's close ties to corporate elites in the oil and gas industry, particularly given the frequency with which industry representatives had lobbied government officials.

The COVID-19 pandemic further exposed the government's close relationship with corporate interests, as large corporations, particularly in the airline and energy sectors, received substantial financial support from the federal government. These bailouts, which critics argued were granted without sufficient conditions or oversight, reinforced concerns that the government was more focused on protecting corporate elites than ensuring that public funds were used in the best interests of all Canadians.

The Patterns of Favoritism: A Recurring Theme

The recurring patterns of favoritism and conflicts of interest within Trudeau's government point to a broader issue of political expediency and a willingness to prioritize the interests of allies, family members, and corporate elites over transparency, fairness, and accountability. These ethical lapses have damaged Trudeau's image as a progressive leader committed to fairness and integrity, and have raised serious questions about the extent to which personal and political connections shape decision-making within his administration.

In each of these controversies, the Trudeau government's actions appeared to benefit powerful interests, whether through shielding a corporation from criminal prosecution, awarding a lucrative contract to an organization with ties to the Prime Minister's family, or making high-profile appointments based on personal connections rather than merit. These repeated lapses in judgment suggest a culture within the government that often places personal relationships and political gain above ethical considerations.

Justin Trudeau's government has been plagued by a series of ethical controversies, many of which involve allegations of favoritism, conflicts of interest, and preferential treatment for corporate elites and political insiders. From the SNC-Lavalin affair to the WE Charity scandal, Trudeau's administration has consistently faced accusations of placing personal connections and political considerations above the public interest.

These repeated ethical lapses have not only damaged Trudeau's credibility but have also raised broader concerns about the integrity of Canada's political system and the influence of corporate and political elites on government decision-making. While Trudeau has sought to position himself as a champion of transparency and fairness, the patterns of favoritism within his government suggest that there is a significant gap between the image he projects and the actions of his administration.

Chapter 7: Media Manipulation and Censorship

Justin Trudeau's Funding of Mainstream Media Outlets: Ensuring Favorable Coverage and Suppression of Dissent

One of the most controversial aspects of Justin Trudeau's tenure as Prime Minister has been the perception that his government has used taxpayer funds to influence and control the narrative presented by mainstream media outlets in Canada. The Trudeau government's media bailout package, introduced in 2018, provided nearly $600 million in subsidies to Canadian media organizations, ostensibly to support journalism and ensure the survival of independent media in an increasingly digital age. However, critics argue that this funding has compromised the independence of the press, ensuring favorable coverage of the Trudeau government while suppressing dissenting voices and critical analysis.

The bailout raised serious concerns about media independence and freedom of the press in Canada. It has been suggested that Trudeau's financial support of the mainstream media has created an environment in which critical coverage of the government is muted, leading to a media landscape where dissent is suppressed and Trudeau's administration is presented in a consistently positive light.

The Media Bailout: A Lifeline or a Conflict of Interest?

In 2018, the Trudeau government announced a $595 million media bailout package aimed at supporting struggling Canadian journalism outlets. The bailout, which was spread over five years, provided tax credits to media organizations and journalists, as well as funding for news organizations to maintain or expand their coverage. The government framed the bailout as a necessary measure to save Canada's media industry, which was facing severe financial difficulties due to the rise of digital media and declining revenues from traditional advertising.

While the intent of the media bailout was presented as preserving Canadian journalism, the move was met with widespread criticism. Opponents of the bailout argued that providing financial support to media outlets created a conflict of interest, particularly given the timing of the bailout, which came ahead of the 2019 federal election. Critics contended that the funding would compromise the independence of the media, as outlets would be reluctant to publish stories critical of the government for fear of losing their financial lifeline.

Additionally, concerns were raised about how the funds would be allocated and who would be responsible for determining which media outlets qualified for the bailout. The creation of a government-appointed independent panel to oversee the distribution of funds raised alarm, as critics questioned whether media organizations that were more favorable to the Trudeau government would be prioritized over those that were more critical.

The Influence of Government Funding on Media Coverage

The key concern surrounding the media bailout is the perception that it has resulted in more favorable media coverage of Justin Trudeau and his government, while discouraging criticism. Media organizations that are financially dependent on government support are less likely to engage in hard-hitting investigative journalism that scrutinizes the actions of the Trudeau government. The fear of losing funding has been cited as a potential reason why certain media outlets have downplayed or ignored scandals and controversies involving Trudeau.

For example, during the **SNC-Lavalin affair**, much of the Canadian mainstream media coverage appeared to downplay the seriousness of the scandal, focusing instead on Trudeau's arguments about protecting jobs rather than the ethical violations at the heart of the controversy. Similarly, during the **WE Charity scandal**, media coverage was criticized for being relatively tame, with some outlets portraying Trudeau's involvement in the controversy as a misunderstanding rather than a deliberate conflict of interest.

Critics argue that this pattern of favorable coverage can be traced back to the financial dependence created by the media bailout. Although the bailout was intended to support independent journalism, it has created a situation in which the press is less inclined to challenge the government or report on stories that could damage Trudeau's political standing.

Suppression of Dissenting Voices

In addition to concerns about favorable coverage, there are also growing fears that Trudeau's government has actively contributed to the suppression of dissenting voices within the Canadian media landscape. Independent media outlets and alternative news sources that have been critical of Trudeau's government have often found themselves marginalized or ignored by the mainstream press, which has been bolstered by the government's funding.

This suppression is evident in the growing divide between mainstream media outlets that receive government subsidies and independent outlets that rely on alternative revenue sources, such as crowdfunding or subscriber-based models. Independent outlets, which tend to be more critical of government actions, have raised alarms about the chilling effect that the media bailout has had on free speech and press freedom in Canada. These outlets argue that the government's financial influence over mainstream media has led to the sidelining of alternative viewpoints, particularly those that challenge the Trudeau government's policies on issues like climate change, free speech, and corporate favoritism.

Moreover, the government's increased control over public broadcasting, particularly through the CBC (Canadian Broadcasting Corporation), has led to further concerns about the suppression of dissent. The CBC, which receives significant government funding, has been accused of bias in its coverage of Trudeau's administration, with critics arguing that its reporting is often favorable toward the government and dismissive of opposition parties and alternative perspectives.

The Impact on Public Trust in Media

The long-term impact of the media bailout on public trust in Canadian journalism has been significant. A growing number of Canadians have expressed concerns about media bias and the lack of critical reporting on the government, particularly when it comes to issues involving Justin Trudeau. This erosion of trust has led to a rise in alternative media outlets and independent journalism, as more Canadians seek out news sources that are not financially tied to the government.

The perception that Trudeau's government is using taxpayer funds to influence media coverage has fueled a broader debate about the role of government in supporting journalism. While proponents of the bailout argue that it is necessary to preserve a free and independent press, critics contend that the bailout has done the opposite, creating a media landscape that is more dependent on government support and less willing to engage in rigorous scrutiny of those in power.

This erosion of public trust has been exacerbated by Trudeau's own handling of ethical scandals. The SNC-Lavalin affair, the WE Charity controversy, and other issues have led many Canadians to question whether they can trust media outlets that appear to be downplaying or ignoring the government's ethical lapses. This growing distrust in the mainstream press has created an environment where alternative media outlets, many of which are critical of Trudeau, have gained prominence.

The Trudeau government's $600 million media bailout has created a perception that mainstream media outlets in Canada are financially beholden to the government and less likely to engage in critical reporting on issues that could damage Trudeau's political standing. While the bailout was framed as a necessary measure to support struggling journalism, its effects have raised serious concerns about media independence, favoritism, and the suppression of dissenting voices.

The pattern of favorable coverage that has emerged since the bailout was implemented, coupled with the lack of aggressive reporting on major government scandals, suggests that the financial influence of Trudeau's administration may be shaping how the Canadian public receives information. At the same time, independent media outlets that refuse government funding have increasingly found themselves marginalized, further exacerbating the divide between government-supported media and alternative news sources.

The long-term consequences of this shift in the media landscape remain to be seen, but the erosion of public trust in the press and the rise of alternative media point to a growing dissatisfaction with the role of government in shaping journalism. The Trudeau government's media bailout has undoubtedly reshaped Canadian journalism, but at what cost to press freedom, transparency, and the public's ability to hold their leaders accountable?

Exploring the Erosion of Free Press Under Justin Trudeau's Leadership and How His Government Silenced Critics

Justin Trudeau's government has faced repeated accusations of undermining free press in Canada, especially through direct funding of media outlets, regulatory changes, and attempts to silence critical voices. Since coming into office in 2015, Trudeau's administration has been accused of shaping public discourse by fostering a media landscape favorable to the government while sidelining dissenting voices, a trend that has raised concerns about the integrity of free press and freedom of expression in the country.

The erosion of free press in Canada is evidenced by multiple actions taken by the Trudeau government, including a multi-million-dollar media bailout that critics argue has compromised media independence, attempts to stifle alternative news sources that provide critical coverage, and policies that threaten the very foundations of journalistic freedom. These moves, which have taken place over the past several years, reveal a worrying trend toward media manipulation and suppression of dissent, raising concerns about the overall health of democracy in Canada.

Media Bailouts: Compromising Journalistic Independence

One of the most significant actions taken by the Trudeau government that critics argue has compromised free press was the introduction of a $595 million media bailout in 2018. The bailout, which was intended to support struggling journalism organizations in the face of declining revenues and digital competition, offered tax credits and other financial incentives to qualifying media outlets. While the bailout was presented as a lifeline for independent journalism, many argued that it created a conflict of interest, as media outlets that relied on government funding might be less inclined to offer critical coverage of the government's actions.

The creation of a panel to oversee which organizations would qualify for the funding raised further concerns about bias and favoritism. The panel was comprised of industry leaders who had close ties to the government, which led to accusations that the selection process would favor pro-government media outlets over those critical of the Trudeau administration. While proponents of the bailout argued that it was necessary to save Canadian journalism, critics suggested that it allowed Trudeau's government to exert undue influence over the press by creating financial dependence.

The bailout's impact on media independence became especially apparent during key political moments, such as the SNC-Lavalin and WE Charity scandals, where much of the mainstream Canadian media downplayed or ignored significant aspects of the controversies. This led to further suspicions that the media's favorable coverage of Trudeau was influenced by their reliance on government subsidies.

Suppression of Dissenting Voices and Alternative Media

In addition to concerns about the media bailout, Trudeau's government has been accused of actively suppressing dissenting voices, particularly those from alternative media outlets. These independent outlets often provide critical perspectives on government policies and actions, challenging the mainstream narrative that tends to be more favorable to the Trudeau administration.

Independent media, including platforms such as Rebel News, True North, and The Post Millennial, have frequently criticized the Trudeau government's handling of key issues, including immigration policy, COVID-19 restrictions, and the handling of corporate corruption scandals. However, these outlets have faced marginalization, legal challenges, and restricted access to government events. Rebel News, for example, was repeatedly denied media accreditation for government press conferences and events, a move that critics argue was an attempt to silence critical reporting on Trudeau's policies. Rebel News eventually won a legal case in 2021, with a Federal Court ruling that Trudeau's government had unfairly discriminated against the outlet by denying it access.

Moreover, alternative media outlets have raised concerns that the Trudeau government's funding of mainstream media outlets has further marginalized independent voices, as government-subsidized outlets dominate the media landscape. This has contributed to an environment in which critical, dissenting perspectives are sidelined, limiting the diversity of voices and viewpoints in the Canadian media.

Attacks on Free Speech: Controversial Policies and Legislation

The Trudeau government has also been criticized for introducing policies and legislation that critics say threaten free speech in Canada. One of the most controversial examples is **Bill C-10**, a proposed update to the Broadcasting Act that aimed to regulate online platforms like Netflix, YouTube, and social media companies. While the government argued that the bill was necessary to ensure Canadian content received proper promotion on digital platforms, free speech advocates warned that it could lead to government overreach in regulating what Canadians could say or share online.

Critics argued that the bill gave the government too much power to control online speech and content, especially as it proposed regulating individual user-generated content on social media platforms. Although some amendments were made to the bill in response to public outcry, the lingering perception was that Trudeau's government was more interested in regulating and controlling online discourse than protecting the freedom of expression.

Bill C-36, introduced in 2021, similarly stoked fears about free speech in Canada. The bill was designed to address online hate speech and harassment, but many civil liberties advocates raised concerns that it could be used to silence critics of the government. The bill proposed new penalties for individuals deemed to have engaged in "hate propaganda" or "hate speech" online, but critics pointed out the potential for abuse, arguing that the government could use such legislation to target and suppress political opposition or dissent.

The Role of CBC: Government-Funded Public Broadcasting and Allegations of Bias

The **Canadian Broadcasting Corporation (CBC)**, which is publicly funded by the federal government, has also been criticized for its perceived bias in favor of Trudeau's administration. While the CBC is supposed to operate independently of government influence, critics argue that its reliance on government funding has resulted in a lack of critical reporting on Trudeau and his policies.

CBC's coverage of key political issues, including government scandals like SNC-Lavalin and WE Charity, has often been viewed as overly favorable to Trudeau. This perception of bias has further fueled concerns about the influence of government funding on the media and the erosion of free press in Canada. Opponents of the government's media funding argue that the CBC, as a publicly funded broadcaster, should be held to a higher standard of independence, but that its coverage consistently aligns with the government's agenda.

Furthermore, the CBC's prominent role in the Canadian media landscape gives the government significant control over the dissemination of information. Critics have pointed out that as a major news source funded by the government, the CBC is in a position to shape public opinion in ways that may protect the government's image while downplaying or ignoring dissenting voices.

Under Justin Trudeau's leadership, the erosion of free press in Canada has been a significant concern for those who value independent journalism and freedom of expression. Through a combination of direct financial support to media outlets, legal challenges to independent media, and the introduction of controversial legislation, Trudeau's government has created an environment in which critical voices are marginalized, and dissent is increasingly difficult to express.

While the media bailout and public broadcasting subsidies have provided financial stability to Canadian journalism, they have also raised serious questions about the independence of the press and the influence of government funding on media coverage. At the same time, the marginalization of independent and alternative media, coupled with attempts to regulate online speech, highlights a growing trend of government control over public discourse in Canada.

As these trends continue, concerns about the future of free press and freedom of speech in Canada will likely intensify. For many critics, Trudeau's actions represent a concerted effort to shape the narrative in his favor, suppress dissenting voices, and control the flow of information—a development that poses a serious threat to the country's democratic institutions.

Chapter 8: The Great Reset and Globalist Agendas

Justin Trudeau's Alignment with Globalist Organizations like the World Economic Forum and the UN: Pushing Policies that Prioritize Global Governance over Canadian Sovereignty

Justin Trudeau's leadership has been characterized by his close alignment with globalist organizations such as the World Economic Forum (WEF) and the United Nations (UN), which has raised concerns about his commitment to Canadian sovereignty. Critics argue that Trudeau's government, through its policies and partnerships with these organizations, has increasingly prioritized global governance, environmental and social justice agendas, and multinational interests over the specific needs and autonomy of Canada and its citizens. These concerns are rooted in Trudeau's frequent participation in globalist initiatives and his administration's efforts to implement policies that are often seen as being aligned with the goals of these international bodies, such as open borders, environmental regulation, and economic restructuring.

Trudeau's Close Ties with the World Economic Forum (WEF)

The **World Economic Forum** is a global organization that brings together political, business, and civil society leaders annually in Davos, Switzerland, to discuss major global challenges, including climate change, economic inequality, and technological innovation. Over the years, Trudeau has been a frequent participant at the WEF meetings, where he has echoed many of the organization's key themes, such as inclusive growth, sustainability, and the transition to a "green economy." His close association with the WEF, particularly its founder Klaus Schwab, has drawn sharp criticism from those who believe that the WEF's agenda undermines national sovereignty by promoting policies that cater to multinational corporations and a global elite.

Critics point to the **Great Reset**, a WEF initiative that seeks to reshape global economies in the wake of the COVID-19 pandemic, as a key example of Trudeau's alignment with globalist goals. The Great Reset proposes leveraging the pandemic as an opportunity to transition to a more sustainable and equitable global economic system, involving increased regulation of industries, greater reliance on public-private partnerships, and a focus on environmental, social, and governance (ESG) goals. While Trudeau has not explicitly endorsed the Great Reset in its entirety, his government's policies on climate change, carbon taxation, and the reimagining of economic systems align closely with the WEF's vision.

Critics argue that by aligning with globalist organizations like the WEF, Trudeau is adopting policies that prioritize global interests—such as fighting climate change, wealth redistribution, and centralized governance—at the expense of Canadian sovereignty and economic self-determination. These policies, according to detractors, weaken Canada's national identity and economic autonomy, making the country more reliant on global supply chains, multinational corporations, and international regulatory frameworks.

United Nations (UN) and Trudeau's Globalist Agenda

Trudeau's alignment with the **United Nations** is another significant aspect of his globalist leanings. Trudeau has been a vocal supporter of many UN initiatives, particularly those related to **climate change**, **migration**, and **human rights**, which has positioned Canada as a leader on the global stage. His government has signed onto various UN agreements, such as the **Paris Climate Agreement** and the **Global Compact for Migration**, further solidifying his reputation as a globalist leader.

The **Paris Climate Agreement**, which was ratified by Canada under Trudeau's leadership, commits signatories to limit global temperature increases by reducing greenhouse gas emissions. While the agreement has been praised by environmentalists, critics argue that the commitments made under the Paris Agreement impose significant economic burdens on Canadian industries and workers, particularly in the energy sector. The introduction of carbon taxes, the cancellation of major pipeline projects, and other regulatory measures meant to reduce emissions have been seen as Trudeau prioritizing international climate obligations over Canada's economic interests.

Similarly, the **Global Compact for Migration**, a non-binding UN agreement, seeks to provide a framework for safe, orderly, and regular migration. Trudeau's endorsement of the Compact has been criticized for undermining Canada's sovereignty by effectively limiting the country's ability to control its own borders. The Compact's focus on facilitating migration and providing protections for migrants has led some critics to argue that it could increase the pressure on Canada's social services and housing markets, particularly in the face of rising immigration levels. These concerns are tied to a broader critique that Trudeau's globalist agenda often caters to international norms and values rather than the specific needs and preferences of Canadian citizens.

Global Governance and Loss of Canadian Sovereignty

Trudeau's commitment to globalist institutions and policies, particularly in the realms of climate change and migration, has contributed to a growing concern that Canada's sovereignty is being eroded in favor of global governance. These concerns center around the idea that by adhering to international agreements and adopting policies aligned with organizations like the UN and WEF, Trudeau is prioritizing globalist goals over the sovereignty and self-determination of Canada.

The **climate change agenda**, for instance, has been a key area where critics argue Trudeau has sacrificed Canadian interests in favor of meeting global obligations. The introduction of a national **carbon tax**, the banning of plastic products, and the push for a transition to renewable energy are all policies that align with global environmental goals, but critics argue that they disproportionately harm Canadian industries—particularly the oil and gas sector. The transition away from fossil fuels has been viewed by many as damaging to Canada's energy independence, forcing the country to rely more heavily on foreign energy sources.

On the issue of **immigration**, critics point to Trudeau's liberal immigration policies as evidence of his alignment with the UN's global migration agenda. Trudeau's government has set ambitious immigration targets, welcoming over 400,000 new immigrants annually. While Trudeau's pro-immigration stance is in line with globalist ideals of open borders and multiculturalism, critics argue that the rapid increase in immigration places a strain on Canada's housing market, social services, and job market. The concern is that these policies are being driven by globalist priorities rather than the best interests of Canada.

Trudeau's "Post-National" Vision of Canada

Trudeau's globalist alignment is perhaps most evident in his **"post-national" vision of Canada**, a phrase he used during an interview in 2015, where he suggested that Canada has no core identity or national identity. This statement, which has been widely criticized, reflects a broader globalist philosophy that rejects the importance of national borders and national sovereignty in favor of a more interconnected and borderless world. Critics argue that Trudeau's globalist rhetoric undermines Canada's unique national identity, culture, and values, and instead promotes a homogenized global vision.

By positioning Canada as a global leader on issues like climate change, human rights, and migration, Trudeau has embraced a worldview that prioritizes international collaboration and governance over national autonomy. His government's policies often reflect this worldview, with critics accusing him of using Canada as a platform to push a broader globalist agenda rather than addressing the specific concerns of Canadians.

Justin Trudeau's government has consistently aligned itself with globalist organizations like the World Economic Forum and the United Nations, adopting policies that critics argue prioritize global governance over Canadian sovereignty. Through initiatives like the Paris Climate Agreement, the Global Compact for Migration, and his participation in WEF-led discussions on the Great Reset, Trudeau has embraced a globalist vision that critics argue comes at the expense of Canada's national interests.

From climate change policies that burden Canadian industries to immigration policies that strain social services, Trudeau's government is seen by many as overly focused on fulfilling international obligations while neglecting the unique needs of Canadians. For critics of globalism, Trudeau's leadership represents a shift away from national sovereignty and toward a world in which Canada's policies are increasingly dictated by international organizations and global elites.

How Justin Trudeau's Government's Decisions Mirror the Global Elite's Agenda, Undermining National Interests

Critics of Justin Trudeau's government have frequently pointed out how his administration's policies align with globalist agendas, particularly those advocated by elite organizations like the World Economic Forum (WEF) and the United Nations (UN). Trudeau's policies on issues like climate change, immigration, and economic restructuring are seen as reflecting the interests and goals of a global elite, often at the expense of Canada's national sovereignty, economic independence, and the well-being of its citizens. This alignment has raised concerns that Trudeau's government is more focused on advancing the global agenda than on safeguarding Canada's distinct interests and identity.

Climate Change and Environmental Policies: A Globalist Agenda

One of the clearest examples of how Trudeau's government mirrors the global elite's agenda is its climate change and environmental policies, which closely align with the priorities of the **World Economic Forum** and the **Paris Climate Agreement**, an initiative led by the **United Nations Framework Convention on Climate Change (UNFCCC)**. While these global initiatives are framed as necessary to combat climate change, critics argue that the policies adopted by Trudeau's government harm Canada's economic interests, particularly in the energy sector.

Trudeau's decision to introduce a **national carbon tax** is a cornerstone of his environmental policy, aimed at reducing greenhouse gas emissions in line with the goals set by the Paris Climate Agreement. However, the carbon tax has been criticized for disproportionately affecting key sectors of Canada's economy, particularly the oil and gas industry, which is a major driver of jobs and economic activity, especially in provinces like Alberta and Saskatchewan. By imposing heavy costs on carbon emissions, the government has made it more difficult for Canadian industries to remain competitive globally, as they face higher operating costs compared to countries that have not adopted similar measures.

Furthermore, the cancellation of projects like the **Keystone XL Pipeline** and other energy infrastructure developments has been seen as a direct concession to the global environmental agenda, with little regard for the economic consequences for Canada. These decisions have effectively restricted the growth of Canada's energy sector, leading to job losses, economic downturns in energy-producing regions, and greater reliance on foreign oil imports, particularly from countries with less stringent environmental regulations. Critics argue that by aligning so closely with global environmental goals, Trudeau has sacrificed Canada's energy independence and undermined its national interests.

Immigration Policies: Fulfilling the UN's Global Compact for Migration

Another area where Trudeau's government's decisions align with the global elite's agenda is in its immigration policies. In 2018, Canada became a signatory to the **Global Compact for Migration**, a UN-led framework that promotes safe, orderly, and regular migration across borders. While the Compact is non-binding, Trudeau's government has enthusiastically embraced its principles, advocating for open and inclusive immigration policies that critics argue put global ideals ahead of the country's national security and economic stability.

Trudeau's government has set ambitious immigration targets, welcoming over **400,000 new immigrants annually**, with the goal of increasing Canada's population to 100 million by 2100. Proponents of these policies argue that immigration is necessary to address labor shortages and aging demographics, but critics contend that such policies strain Canada's social services, housing market, and job market. The influx of new immigrants has led to skyrocketing housing prices in major cities like Toronto and Vancouver, exacerbating affordability issues for Canadian citizens. Additionally, concerns have been raised about the impact of mass immigration on Canadian identity, culture, and national security.

The alignment with the **UN's Global Compact for Migration** reflects a broader trend of globalist thinking, where national borders are seen as less important than promoting the free movement of people and fostering multiculturalism. However, critics argue that Trudeau's approach to immigration prioritizes global goals over the well-being and cohesion of Canadian society, undermining national sovereignty in the process.

Economic Restructuring and the "Great Reset"

Trudeau's economic policies have also been seen as aligning with the **World Economic Forum's (WEF)**

Great Reset, an initiative that calls for a fundamental rethinking of capitalism in the wake of the COVID-19 pandemic. The Great Reset proposes restructuring economies to prioritize sustainability, social justice, and environmental stewardship over profit-driven growth. Trudeau has echoed many of these themes in his own policy speeches, and his government has introduced measures that critics argue mirror the WEF's globalist agenda.

For example, during a speech at the United Nations in September 2020, Trudeau stated, "This pandemic has provided an opportunity for a reset." His government has since embraced policies aimed at rethinking the role of government in the economy, including increasing public spending, expanding social safety nets, and promoting green energy projects as part of Canada's recovery from the pandemic. Critics argue that while these policies may align with the Great Reset's vision of a more equitable and sustainable world, they undermine Canada's economic sovereignty by increasing government control over industries and reducing the country's reliance on traditional, wealth-generating sectors like oil and gas.

The push for a **"green economy"** has been particularly controversial, as it has led to the sidelining of Canada's natural resources sector in favor of renewable energy projects that are not yet economically viable on a large scale. Critics argue that Trudeau's economic policies are more in line with the WEF's globalist vision than with Canada's immediate economic needs, as they prioritize long-term sustainability goals over job creation and economic growth.

The "Post-National" Vision of Canada

Trudeau's globalist leanings are also reflected in his **"post-national" vision** of Canada. In a 2015 interview with The New York Times, Trudeau stated that Canada had "no core identity," suggesting that the country's strength lies in its diversity and openness to the world. This statement, which has been widely criticized, reflects a broader rejection of traditional notions of national identity and sovereignty in favor of a more globalist perspective that aligns with the values of elite international organizations like the UN and WEF.

Critics argue that Trudeau's **post-national vision** undermines the idea of Canada as a sovereign nation with its own distinct culture, values, and interests. By promoting policies that emphasize multiculturalism, open borders, and global cooperation, Trudeau is seen as diluting Canada's national identity and weakening its ability to chart an independent course on the global stage. This approach, according to detractors, makes Canada more susceptible to the influence of global elites and international organizations, undermining its sovereignty and autonomy.

Centralization of Power and Global Governance

Another way Trudeau's government has mirrored the global elite's agenda is through the **centralization of**

power within the federal government, a move that critics argue aligns with globalist preferences for top-down governance rather than decentralized, locally accountable leadership. Trudeau's government has expanded its control over areas traditionally governed by the provinces, such as healthcare, education, and energy, under the guise of promoting national standards and addressing global challenges.

The imposition of federal carbon taxes, for example, has been seen as an encroachment on provincial jurisdiction, particularly in provinces like Alberta, which have traditionally relied on their natural resource industries. This centralization of power is in line with the globalist agenda of creating uniform policies that can be more easily aligned with international standards, but it has raised concerns about the erosion of provincial autonomy and the ability of local governments to pursue policies that are in their best interests.

Justin Trudeau's government has consistently aligned itself with the global elite's agenda, implementing policies that critics argue prioritize global governance, environmental and social justice, and economic restructuring over Canada's national interests. From climate change initiatives to immigration policies and economic restructuring, Trudeau's decisions mirror the goals of organizations like the World Economic Forum and the United Nations, leading to concerns that his government is undermining Canadian sovereignty in favor of a globalist vision.

By adopting policies that emphasize global cooperation, sustainability, and open borders, Trudeau has positioned Canada as a leader on the world stage, but critics argue that this leadership comes at a cost. The erosion of Canada's energy independence, the strain on social services from mass immigration, and the centralization of power in Ottawa all point to a government that is more focused on fulfilling global obligations than on addressing the specific needs of Canadians.

Part III: A Legacy of Division and Betrayal

Chapter 9: East vs. West – A Trudeau Tradition

How Both Pierre and Justin Trudeau's Policies Fueled Resentment in Western Canada: From the

National Energy Program to Carbon Taxes and Resource Blockades

Western Canada, particularly Alberta and Saskatchewan, has long been at odds with federal policies that it perceives as catering to the interests of central and eastern Canada, often at the expense of its own economy and prosperity. This tension between the western provinces and the federal government has been significantly exacerbated by the policies of both Pierre Elliott Trudeau and his son, Justin Trudeau. Both leaders have implemented policies that have profoundly affected Western Canada's resource-rich economy, particularly its oil and gas sector, resulting in deep resentment and a growing sense of alienation in the region.

Pierre Trudeau's **National Energy Program (NEP)** in the 1980s is widely seen as the starting point for this resentment, while Justin Trudeau's **carbon tax**, **pipeline cancellations**, and **environmental regulations** have further inflamed tensions. These policies are perceived by many in the West as undermining the region's economic potential, contributing to a long-standing sense of being economically exploited by Ottawa in favor of central Canadian interests.

Pierre Trudeau's National Energy Program (NEP): A Flashpoint for Western Alienation

Pierre Trudeau's **National Energy Program (NEP)**, introduced in 1980, is often regarded as one of the most divisive policies in Canadian history, particularly from the perspective of Western Canada. The NEP was introduced in response to the global oil crisis of the 1970s and was intended to make Canada energy self-sufficient, while also redistributing wealth from the oil-rich West to the rest of the country. However, the program had devastating economic consequences for Alberta, which was heavily reliant on its oil and gas industry.

The NEP included several key measures that were seen as highly detrimental to Alberta's economy:

- **Price controls on oil**, which kept Canadian oil prices artificially low compared to world prices, reducing profits for oil producers in Alberta.
- **Increased federal control over energy resources**, which was viewed as an intrusion on provincial jurisdiction and an attempt to centralize power in Ottawa.
- **Revenue-sharing mechanisms**, such as the Petroleum and Gas Revenue Tax, which diverted a portion of Alberta's oil revenues to the federal government, ostensibly to benefit the rest of the country.

The NEP was deeply unpopular in Alberta, where it was seen as an economic attack on the province. The program led to widespread job losses, bankruptcies in the oil industry, and a significant economic downturn in the region. The resentment generated by the NEP gave rise to the sentiment of **Western alienation**, the belief that the federal government prioritizes the interests of central and eastern Canada while neglecting or actively harming the West. This sense of alienation has persisted for decades and continues to shape the political landscape of Western Canada.

Justin Trudeau's Carbon Tax and Environmental Policies: Reinforcing Western Alienation

Justin Trudeau's government has exacerbated the resentment that began with his father's National Energy Program through its own set of policies that disproportionately impact Western Canada's resource-based economy. Chief among these is the **national carbon tax**, introduced as part of the Liberal government's strategy to combat climate change and reduce Canada's greenhouse gas emissions in line with international agreements like the **Paris Climate Accord**.

The carbon tax places a price on carbon emissions, forcing businesses and consumers to pay for the carbon dioxide they release into the atmosphere. While the Trudeau government framed this policy as an essential step toward addressing climate change, it has been met with fierce opposition in Alberta and Saskatchewan, where the economy is heavily dependent on oil, gas, and other carbon-intensive industries. Critics argue that the carbon tax disproportionately affects Western Canada by making energy production more expensive, leading to job losses in the oil and gas sector, higher energy costs for consumers, and reduced economic growth in the region.

The sense of betrayal felt in the West is further compounded by Trudeau's **environmental regulations** and **pipeline decisions**. Trudeau's government has canceled or delayed several major pipeline projects, including the **Northern Gateway Pipeline** and **Energy East**, while also placing heavy regulatory burdens on the oil sands. The inability to get pipelines built has left Alberta's oil industry struggling to get its product to international markets, contributing to bottlenecks, lower oil prices for Canadian producers, and an overall sense that the federal government is actively working against the interests of Western Canada.

At the same time, Trudeau's approval of the **Trans Mountain Pipeline expansion** has not alleviated Western frustrations, as it was seen as a grudging concession rather than a genuine effort to support the region's economic growth. The project faced numerous delays, protests, and legal challenges, and even after its approval, many in the West felt that the federal government had failed to adequately defend the project against opposition from environmentalists and certain provincial governments, such as British Columbia.

Resource Blockades and Economic Consequences

In addition to Trudeau's environmental policies, the issue of **resource blockades** has been a major point of contention between Western Canada and the federal government. Throughout Trudeau's time in office, resource blockades—often led by Indigenous groups or environmental activists—have disrupted pipeline projects, natural gas extraction, and other resource development initiatives. These blockades have added to the perception that the federal government is either unwilling or unable to protect Western Canada's economic interests.

For example, in 2020, blockades across Canada halted rail transport in solidarity with the Wet'suwet'en hereditary chiefs, who opposed the construction of the **Coastal GasLink pipeline** in British Columbia. The blockades caused widespread economic disruption, particularly in Western Canada, as they delayed shipments of goods and resources. The federal government's response was seen as weak, as Trudeau emphasized dialogue and reconciliation with Indigenous groups rather than taking swift action to end the blockades.

From the perspective of many in Western Canada, the federal government's handling of these blockades reflects a lack of concern for the region's economic well-being. The failure to ensure the smooth development of energy infrastructure and the repeated delays to resource projects have left Western Canadians feeling that their economic interests are being sacrificed to appease environmentalists and other political factions that are more influential in Ottawa and central Canada.

The Political Fallout: Rise of Wexit and Western Alienation

The resentment fueled by both Pierre and Justin Trudeau's policies has contributed to the rise of **Western separatist movements**, most notably the **Wexit** movement, which advocates for the independence of Alberta and other western provinces from the rest of Canada. While Wexit remains a fringe movement, it reflects a growing sense of alienation and frustration in the West, where many feel that the federal government has consistently failed to represent their interests.

This sense of alienation has been further reflected in federal election results, where the Liberal Party under Justin Trudeau has struggled to gain support in Alberta, Saskatchewan, and other western provinces. In the 2019 and 2021 federal elections, the Liberal Party was almost entirely shut out of Alberta and Saskatchewan, where the **Conservative Party** remains dominant. The electoral divide between the West and the rest of Canada has only deepened under Trudeau's leadership, reinforcing the perception that Western Canada's concerns are being ignored by the federal government.

The policies of both Pierre and Justin Trudeau have contributed to a deep and lasting sense of resentment in Western Canada. Pierre Trudeau's National Energy Program in the 1980s is still remembered as an economic attack on Alberta, and Justin Trudeau's carbon tax, pipeline cancellations, and environmental regulations have reinforced the perception that Ottawa is more interested in placating environmentalists and central Canadian voters than supporting the West's economic interests.

The rise of separatist sentiment and Western alienation under Justin Trudeau's government reflects a broader dissatisfaction with a federal government that many Western Canadians feel has consistently prioritized the interests of central and eastern Canada over their own. As long as policies that harm the West's resource-based economy continue, this resentment is likely to persist, making Western alienation a long-term challenge for Canadian unity.

Analyzing the Rise of Movements Like Wexit and Alberta Separatism as a Direct Result of Trudeau-Family Policies

The rise of separatist movements such as **Wexit** (Western Exit) and Alberta separatism can be traced directly to policies implemented by both Pierre and Justin Trudeau. These movements are a manifestation of long-standing resentment in Western Canada, especially Alberta, where many feel that federal policies have consistently prioritized the interests of central and eastern Canada at the expense of the West. This sense of alienation has been fueled by economic policies, such as Pierre Trudeau's **National Energy Program (NEP)** in the 1980s, and environmental and taxation measures under Justin Trudeau's leadership, including the **carbon tax** and **pipeline cancellations**. These policies have disproportionately affected the resource-rich economy of Western Canada, particularly the oil and gas sector, leading to a growing sense of political and economic marginalization in the region.

The Roots of Western Alienation: Pierre Trudeau's National Energy Program (NEP)

Western alienation is not a new phenomenon. It dates back to the early 20th century but was significantly exacerbated by Pierre Trudeau's **National Energy Program (NEP)**, introduced in 1980. The NEP was designed to increase Canadian energy self-sufficiency, redistribute wealth from Alberta's booming oil sector to the rest of Canada, and exert greater federal control over energy resources. However, it had devastating economic consequences for Alberta and is widely regarded as the point at which Western alienation crystallized into a distinct political identity.

The NEP included measures such as:

- **Price controls on oil**: By keeping oil prices below world market rates, the NEP reduced the profits of Alberta's oil producers, leading to significant economic losses.
- **Revenue-sharing mechanisms**: The NEP introduced new taxes on oil production that redirected revenue from Alberta to the federal government.
- **Increased federal control**: The program encroached on provincial jurisdiction, heightening tensions between Alberta and Ottawa.

The NEP was viewed in Alberta as an economic attack by the federal government, designed to benefit central and eastern Canada at the expense of the West. It resulted in massive job losses, bankruptcies, and economic stagnation in Alberta's oil industry. This deepened the sense of alienation and resentment toward Ottawa, setting the stage for future conflicts between Western Canada and the federal government.

Justin Trudeau's Carbon Tax and Environmental Policies: Reigniting Western Alienation

Justin Trudeau's government has continued the trend of policies that Western Canadians, particularly in Alberta, view as detrimental to their economic interests. Chief among these is the **national carbon tax**, introduced in 2019 as part of Trudeau's efforts to combat climate change. While the tax was framed as a necessary measure to reduce carbon emissions and meet international climate commitments, it has been fiercely opposed in Alberta and other Western provinces where the economy is heavily dependent on the oil and gas sector.

The carbon tax imposes additional costs on fossil fuel production, making it more expensive for energy companies to operate in Canada. This has had a particularly negative impact on Alberta, which relies on oil and gas production for jobs, government revenue, and economic growth. Critics argue that the carbon tax disproportionately affects Western Canada by increasing energy prices, reducing competitiveness, and contributing to job losses in the resource sector. These economic pressures have reinforced the sense that the federal government, under Justin Trudeau, is indifferent or even hostile to the economic well-being of the West.

Trudeau's environmental policies have also been a major source of contention. His government has canceled or delayed several key energy infrastructure projects, including the **Northern Gateway Pipeline** and **Energy East**, while imposing stricter regulations on oil sands development. The perceived failure to adequately support pipeline projects, such as the **Trans Mountain Pipeline expansion**, has contributed to the feeling in Alberta that Ottawa is prioritizing environmental interests and the demands of other provinces over the economic needs of Western Canada. Many in the West see these policies as part of a broader agenda that seeks to phase out the oil and gas industry, which is the backbone of Alberta's economy.

The Emergence of Wexit and Alberta Separatism

The policies of both Pierre and Justin Trudeau have created fertile ground for the rise of separatist movements in Western Canada. **Wexit**, short for "Western Exit," is a movement that advocates for the separation of the western provinces—primarily Alberta, Saskatchewan, and British Columbia—from Canada. While the movement remains relatively small, its rise reflects the deep frustration and alienation felt by many Western Canadians who believe that their economic and political interests are being systematically ignored by the federal government.

The Wexit movement gained momentum following the 2019 federal election, in which Justin Trudeau's Liberal Party won a minority government despite receiving almost no support from Alberta and Saskatchewan. The election results, in which the Liberal Party was effectively shut out of Alberta and Saskatchewan, reinforced the sense that Western Canada is politically marginalized and underrepresented in Ottawa. The idea of separation became more appealing to those who felt that the region would be better off controlling its own resources and making its own decisions, free from what they perceive as the interference of a distant federal government.

The **Wexit movement** was officially recognized as a federal political party in 2020 under the name **Wexit Canada**, later renamed the **Maverick Party**. While its electoral success has been limited, the party's emergence underscores the growing discontent in Western Canada and the desire for greater autonomy or even independence from Ottawa.

The rise of Alberta separatism has also been fueled by a broader sense of Western alienation, which has been exacerbated by the economic downturn in the oil and gas sector and the perception that federal policies are directly harming the region's economic prospects. Although Alberta separatism is not yet a mainstream political movement, it represents a significant political force that reflects the region's deepening frustration with federal leadership, particularly under the Trudeau family.

Economic and Political Consequences of Separatism

The rise of Wexit and Alberta separatism has had significant political and economic consequences, both for Western Canada and for the country as a whole. Politically, the growing support for separatism has deepened the divide between the federal government and the western provinces, making it more difficult for national unity to be maintained. The sense that Western Canada is being economically exploited to benefit central and eastern Canada, a sentiment that dates back to Pierre Trudeau's NEP, has only intensified under Justin Trudeau's leadership.

Economically, the separatist movements reflect the frustration felt by many Western Canadians over the federal government's handling of resource development and energy infrastructure projects. The inability to get pipelines built, the increased regulatory burden on the oil and gas sector, and the imposition of carbon taxes have all contributed to a growing sense that Alberta and Saskatchewan are being unfairly punished for their reliance on fossil fuels. This has fueled calls for greater provincial autonomy over resource development, with some even advocating for the establishment of a new independent state in the West.

The policies of both Pierre and Justin Trudeau have played a pivotal role in fueling the rise of separatist movements in Western Canada. Pierre Trudeau's National Energy Program set the stage for decades of Western alienation by economically harming Alberta's oil sector and deepening the divide between Ottawa and the West. Justin Trudeau's carbon tax, environmental regulations, and pipeline policies have further exacerbated this alienation, contributing to a growing sense that Western Canada's interests are being sacrificed for the sake of central and eastern Canada.

The rise of Wexit and Alberta separatism is a direct response to these policies, reflecting a broader dissatisfaction with the Trudeau family's approach to governing Canada. As long as these grievances persist, the separatist movements in Western Canada are likely to remain a significant political force, posing a challenge to the unity of the country.

Chapter 10: Destroying Canada's Identity

Cultural Marxism and Social Engineering

How the Trudeau Legacy Has Eroded Canadian Traditions and Identity in Favor of Multiculturalism and Progressive Social Policies

The Trudeau family legacy, marked by the tenures of both Pierre and Justin Trudeau, has played a defining role in reshaping Canadian identity and traditions. Pierre Trudeau, during his time as prime minister, introduced **official multiculturalism** and redefined Canada's relationship with its cultural roots. His son, Justin Trudeau, has further accelerated this transformation through progressive social policies that promote diversity, inclusion, and globalism, often at the expense of traditional Canadian values. Critics argue that the Trudeau legacy has undermined the core identity and historical traditions of Canada, shifting the nation towards a more post-national, multicultural, and progressive framework that prioritizes globalist ideals over national identity and cultural heritage.

Pierre Trudeau's Introduction of Multiculturalism

Pierre Trudeau, who served as Canada's prime minister from 1968 to 1979 and again from 1980 to 1984, is widely credited with laying the foundations for Canada's current identity as a multicultural nation. In 1971, his government introduced the **Multiculturalism Policy**, making Canada the first country in the world to adopt official multiculturalism as a national policy. This policy aimed to recognize and preserve the cultural diversity of Canada's population while promoting the integration of immigrants into Canadian society.

The introduction of multiculturalism was part of a broader effort by Pierre Trudeau to distance Canada from its colonial past and create a national identity that was more inclusive and reflective of the country's diverse population. By emphasizing diversity and promoting the idea that no single cultural or ethnic group should dominate Canadian society, Pierre Trudeau fundamentally altered the national narrative, moving away from a focus on traditional European and Christian values that had previously defined the country.

While multiculturalism was celebrated by many for its inclusivity, it also sparked criticism. Detractors argued that the policy weakened Canadian traditions by de-emphasizing the shared cultural and historical roots of the country. The celebration of ethnic diversity, while valuable, was seen by some as leading to cultural fragmentation, with different groups coexisting without a unifying national identity. Pierre Trudeau's vision of a multicultural Canada was seen by critics as diminishing the significance of Canada's British and French heritage, undermining the country's historical identity.

Justin Trudeau's Post-National Vision: Expanding Multiculturalism and Progressive Policies

Justin Trudeau has expanded upon his father's legacy, further embedding multiculturalism and progressive social policies into the fabric of Canadian society. He has articulated a vision of Canada as a **"post-national state,"** famously stating in a 2015 interview with The New York Times that "there is no core identity, no mainstream in Canada." This statement reflects a broader globalist outlook, where national borders and traditional values are seen as less important than the promotion of diversity, inclusivity, and global cooperation.

Justin Trudeau's embrace of multiculturalism goes hand in hand with his government's progressive policies on immigration, diversity, and social issues. His administration has set ambitious immigration targets, welcoming over **400,000 new immigrants annually** as part of an effort to foster diversity and address labor shortages. Critics, however, argue that this rapid increase in immigration has strained Canada's social services, housing market, and job market, while undermining Canada's cultural cohesion. The focus on promoting multiculturalism at the expense of fostering a unified national identity has led to concerns that Canada's traditions and historical values are being eroded.

Under Justin Trudeau's leadership, Canada has also seen the implementation of **progressive social policies** that promote inclusivity in areas such as gender equality, LGBTQ+ rights, and Indigenous reconciliation. These policies, while widely praised by progressives, have been criticized by some for being divisive and for promoting a liberal social agenda that is out of step with the values of many Canadians. For example, the introduction of **Bill C-16**, which added gender identity and expression to the Canadian Human Rights Act, was seen by critics as an example of overreach, where progressive policies infringe on free speech and traditional values.

Undermining Canadian Traditions: The Decline of Shared Heritage (cont'd)

The Trudeau family's policies on multiculturalism and progressive social issues have contributed to a perception that Canada is losing touch with its historical traditions and shared heritage. Under Pierre Trudeau, the shift towards multiculturalism and away from Canada's colonial past was meant to foster inclusivity, but it also had the unintended consequence of de-emphasizing Canada's British and French roots. These roots were historically seen as central to Canadian identity, particularly through the preservation of traditions such as the monarchy, Christian values, and the use of both French and English as official languages.

Justin Trudeau has expanded on this shift by embracing policies that critics argue further erode Canada's traditional institutions and values. His **post-national vision**, which downplays the importance of a unified national identity, reflects a broader globalist outlook where traditional cultural symbols and practices are seen as less relevant in an increasingly diverse and multicultural society. This has led to concerns that Canada's historical identity is being diluted in favor of promoting diversity at all costs.

For example, some critics argue that Justin Trudeau's government has paid less attention to preserving **Canada's connection to the monarchy**. While the monarchy remains a symbolic figurehead in Canada, the role of the Crown in Canadian culture has been downplayed, reflecting a broader tendency to distance the country from its colonial past. This has fueled debates about whether the monarchy should continue to play a role in Canadian life, with many Canadians, particularly younger generations, seeing it as an outdated institution.

Traditional Christian holidays such as **Christmas** have also seen a decline in their cultural prominence under the Trudeau government, with more inclusive terms like "holiday season" being used in official government messaging. This shift is seen by some as part of a broader effort to accommodate a multicultural population, but it has also sparked criticism from those who feel that Canada's Christian heritage is being erased in favor of a more secular and inclusive agenda.

Multiculturalism vs. National Unity

While multiculturalism is celebrated by many Canadians as a core part of the nation's identity, it has also been criticized for contributing to cultural fragmentation. The emphasis on ethnic and cultural diversity can, in some cases, lead to a weakening of a unified national identity. The idea of a **"mosaic"**—where different cultural and ethnic groups maintain their distinctiveness rather than assimilating into a common Canadian identity—can create challenges for national cohesion. Critics argue that, by focusing on the promotion of individual cultural identities, Canada risks losing the shared values and traditions that once united the country.

One of the key criticisms of the Trudeau family's multicultural policies is that they have shifted the focus from **integration to accommodation**. Under Pierre Trudeau's vision of multiculturalism, the idea was to integrate immigrants into Canadian society while still respecting their cultural heritage. However, under Justin Trudeau, the focus has shifted toward accommodating various cultural practices and beliefs, which some argue has led to increased **cultural enclaves** where newcomers remain separate from the broader Canadian community.

This shift has sparked debates about the balance between respecting diversity and preserving national unity. Critics argue that Justin Trudeau's government has prioritized the former at the expense of the latter, leading to a weakened sense of Canadian identity. The rise of **identity politics** and the emphasis on diversity has, in some cases, created divisions within the country, where different groups compete for recognition and resources, rather than contributing to a cohesive national identity.

Progressive Social Policies and Their Impact on Canadian Traditions

In addition to multiculturalism, Justin Trudeau's government has implemented a range of progressive social policies that have further reshaped Canadian identity. Trudeau's administration has positioned itself as a champion of **diversity and inclusion**, with a focus on advancing **LGBTQ+ rights**, **gender equality**, and **Indigenous reconciliation**. While these policies have been widely praised by progressive advocates, they have also been criticized for contributing to the erosion of traditional values and institutions.

One of the most controversial aspects of Justin Trudeau's progressive agenda is his government's focus on **gender identity and expression**. In 2016, Trudeau's government passed **Bill C-16**, which added gender identity and expression to the **Canadian Human Rights Act** and the **Criminal Code**. The bill was hailed as a victory for transgender rights, but it also sparked a heated debate over free speech and the protection of traditional values. Critics, including academics and religious groups, argued that the bill infringed on freedom of expression by compelling the use of specific gender pronouns, while others saw it as a broader attack on traditional gender roles and family structures.

Similarly, Trudeau's emphasis on **Indigenous reconciliation** has been both celebrated and criticized. While efforts to address historical injustices and improve the relationship between Canada and Indigenous peoples are widely supported, some critics argue that these policies have contributed to the division of Canadian society by prioritizing certain groups over others. The focus on Indigenous reconciliation, along with other progressive policies, is seen by some as part of a broader shift away from the traditions and values that once united Canadians, toward a more fragmented and identity-based society.

Erosion of National Identity: A Post-National State?

At the heart of the criticism leveled against the Trudeau family's policies is the idea that Canada has moved away from having a **cohesive national identity** toward becoming a **post-national state**. The Trudeau vision, particularly under Justin, promotes the idea that Canada's identity is not tied to a single culture, history, or set of values, but rather is an evolving and fluid concept shaped by its diversity. While this may resonate with many in Canada's urban and progressive circles, it has also led to fears that Canada is losing touch with its traditions and heritage.

This "post-national" vision undermines the idea of Canada as a nation-state with distinct values and cultural practices. The promotion of **globalism**, the embrace of **multiculturalism**, and the push for **progressive social policies** have led some critics to argue that Canada is becoming more of a **global experiment** than a country with a unified identity. As a result, traditional symbols of Canadian culture—whether it be the monarchy, Christian holidays, or the values of hard work and self-reliance— have been increasingly de-emphasized in favor of a more fluid, inclusive, and progressive identity.

The Trudeau family's legacy, from Pierre Trudeau's introduction of multiculturalism to Justin Trudeau's post-national vision, has profoundly transformed Canada's identity. While these policies have promoted inclusivity, diversity, and progressivism, they have also contributed to the erosion of traditional Canadian values and the weakening of a cohesive national identity. Critics argue that the focus on diversity and progressive social policies has led to cultural fragmentation, a diminished sense of shared heritage, and a loss of connection to Canada's historical traditions.

The question facing Canada is whether this transformation will continue to foster a more inclusive and diverse society, or whether the erosion of national identity will ultimately undermine the country's unity and cultural coherence. As the Trudeau legacy continues to shape Canada's future, the debate over the balance between preserving traditions and embracing progressivism is likely to remain a central issue in Canadian politics.

The Long-Term Consequences of Pierre and Justin Trudeau's Social Experiments on Canadian Unity

The policies and social experiments introduced by Pierre Trudeau and later expanded by his son, Justin Trudeau, have had profound and lasting impacts on Canadian society. Both leaders have pushed for a vision of Canada that embraces multiculturalism, progressive social policies, and a departure from traditional national values. While these initiatives have been praised by some as forward-thinking and inclusive, they have also sparked deep divisions within Canadian society, leading to significant concerns about the long-term consequences for national unity.

Pierre Trudeau's introduction of **official multiculturalism** and his emphasis on weakening the influence of traditional institutions were bold steps that sought to redefine Canada's national identity. Justin Trudeau's embrace of **progressive social policies**, such as gender identity legislation, expanded immigration, and a "post-national" vision of Canada, further transformed the social landscape. However, these changes have not been without controversy, and critics argue that the Trudeau legacy has weakened the sense of shared identity, exacerbated regional divisions, and contributed to political and cultural polarization in Canada.

The Fragmentation of National Identity

Pierre Trudeau's decision to introduce official **multiculturalism** in 1971 fundamentally altered the course of Canadian identity. The policy aimed to celebrate cultural diversity and promote inclusivity in a way that recognized Canada's growing immigrant population. However, over the long term, it has led to concerns that the emphasis on diversity has come at the cost of a cohesive national identity.

Critics argue that the focus on promoting individual cultural identities has contributed to the fragmentation of Canada's traditional values and institutions. Prior to the implementation of multiculturalism, Canada's identity was shaped largely by its British and French heritage, with institutions such as the monarchy, Christian traditions, and a shared history playing key roles in uniting the country. Pierre Trudeau's multiculturalism policy, while aimed at fostering inclusivity, contributed to the erosion of these unifying elements, as it promoted the idea that no single cultural group should dominate the national narrative.

The long-term result of this policy has been a more fragmented society, where different cultural and ethnic groups coexist without necessarily sharing a common set of values or historical touchstones. While diversity is celebrated, the lack of a unifying national identity has raised concerns about the future of Canadian unity, as different groups may prioritize their own cultural interests over those of the broader national community.

Regional Divisions: Western Alienation and Quebec Sovereignty

Pierre and Justin Trudeau's policies have also contributed to deepening **regional divisions** in Canada, particularly in Western Canada and Quebec. Pierre Trudeau's **National Energy Program (NEP)**, introduced in the 1980s, is often cited as the starting point for modern **Western alienation**. The NEP was viewed by many in Alberta and other western provinces as an attempt by Ottawa to control their energy resources and redistribute wealth to the rest of the country. The program caused lasting resentment in the West and is seen as a key factor in the rise of **Western separatism**, which remains a political force today, especially with movements like **Wexit**.

Justin Trudeau's policies have further exacerbated these regional tensions. His **carbon tax**, environmental regulations, and cancellation of key pipeline projects have been particularly unpopular in Alberta and Saskatchewan, where the economy is heavily dependent on oil and gas production. These policies have been seen as a continuation of the federal government's disregard for Western economic interests, deepening the divide between the West and the rest of the country. The rise of separatist sentiment in Alberta, epitomized by movements like **Wexit**, reflects a growing frustration with what is perceived as federal overreach and a lack of representation for Western Canada in Ottawa.

At the same time, Justin Trudeau's embrace of multiculturalism and progressive social policies has also reignited tensions in **Quebec**, where the province has long sought to preserve its distinct culture and language. The province's movement for sovereignty, which reached its peak in the 1995 referendum, remains a potent political force. Quebec's resistance to certain federal policies, including immigration and multiculturalism, reflects a broader tension between the province's desire to maintain its unique identity and the federal government's push for a more multicultural and progressive vision of Canada.

Political Polarization

The Trudeau family's social experiments have also contributed to increasing **political polarization** in Canada. Both Pierre and Justin Trudeau have promoted a vision of Canada that is deeply rooted in **progressive values**, often at the expense of more traditional or conservative viewpoints. This has created a sharp divide between progressives and conservatives, with the Trudeau family often becoming a focal point for this polarization.

Justin Trudeau's progressive policies on **gender identity**, **LGBTQ+ rights**, **climate change**, and **immigration** have been celebrated by liberals and progressives, but they have also sparked backlash from conservatives, particularly in rural and Western Canada. This polarization is reflected in electoral results, where the **Liberal Party** under Justin Trudeau has dominated in urban centers and in parts of eastern Canada, while the **Conservative Party** has gained increasing support in rural areas and the western provinces.

This divide has led to growing concerns about the **urban-rural divide** in Canada, with urban areas becoming more progressive and diverse, while rural areas remain more conservative and traditional. The result is a more polarized political landscape, where the gap between progressives and conservatives is widening, making it more difficult for national unity to be maintained. The Trudeau family's emphasis on progressive social policies and multiculturalism is seen by some as contributing to this polarization, as it prioritizes certain values over others.

Erosion of Traditional Values and Institutions

Both Pierre and Justin Trudeau's policies have contributed to the **erosion of traditional Canadian values and institutions**, which has led to growing concerns about the long-term implications for national unity. Pierre Trudeau's vision of Canada as a **multicultural society** was designed to distance the country from its colonial past and create a more inclusive society. However, this vision has led to the de-emphasis of traditional symbols and values that once united Canadians, such as the **monarchy**, **Christian traditions**, and the **English-French bicultural framework**.

Justin Trudeau has further expanded on this vision by promoting progressive social policies that emphasize **diversity, inclusion, and globalism**, often at the expense of traditional values. His **post-national vision** of Canada, in which there is "no core identity," reflects a broader effort to redefine Canada's role in the world. However, this approach has led to criticism that Canada is losing its sense of shared heritage and national identity, as it increasingly prioritizes global values over its own cultural and historical traditions.

The result is an ongoing **cultural shift** in Canada, where traditional values and institutions are being replaced by a more fluid and globalist identity. Critics argue that this shift is eroding the sense of national unity, as different regions and cultural groups become more focused on their own interests, rather than on what unites them as Canadians.

The long-term consequences of the social experiments introduced by Pierre and Justin Trudeau have been a profound transformation of Canadian society, but one that has come with significant risks to national unity. While both leaders have promoted **inclusivity, multiculturalism**, and **progressive social policies**, their legacy has also been one of growing **regional divisions, political polarization**, and a sense that Canada's traditional values and institutions are being eroded.

Western alienation, Quebec sovereignty, and political polarization have all been exacerbated by the Trudeau family's policies, leading to concerns that Canada is becoming more divided along regional, cultural, and ideological lines. As the country continues to grapple with these challenges, the question remains whether the Trudeau vision of a multicultural and progressive Canada can coexist with the need for a shared national identity that unites all Canadians

Chapter 11: The Trudeau Family and China

Examining Both Pierre and Justin Trudeau's Relationships with China: From Pierre's Early Diplomatic Ties to Justin's Alleged Favoritism Toward Chinese Interests

The Trudeau family has a long and complex history with China, beginning with **Pierre Trudeau**'s groundbreaking diplomatic efforts in the 1970s, which established Canada as one of the first Western nations to officially recognize the **People's Republic of China (PRC)**. Pierre's relationship with China was rooted in pragmatism and a desire to establish Canada as an independent actor on the global stage, free from the shadow of American foreign policy. His son, **Justin Trudeau**, has continued to build on this relationship, though his tenure as prime minister has been mired in allegations of **favoritism** toward China and accusations that his government has been too accommodating to Chinese interests.

Pierre's diplomatic ties with China were largely seen as a bold move that elevated Canada's global standing, while Justin's relationship with China has been more controversial, with critics accusing him of being too close to the Chinese Communist Party (CCP) and prioritizing Chinese interests over Canada's.

Pierre Trudeau's Early Diplomatic Ties with China

Pierre Trudeau's relationship with China was a pivotal moment in Canadian foreign policy. Before becoming prime minister, Trudeau had visited **Maoist China** in 1949 and again in 1960, during which time he developed a fascination with the country and its revolutionary ideology. His sympathy for certain socialist ideas, combined with his desire to distance Canada from U.S.

dominance in global affairs, set the stage for his later engagement with China.

In 1970, Pierre Trudeau's government made the bold decision to establish formal diplomatic relations with the People's Republic of China, making Canada one of the first Western nations to do so. This move was seen as a significant diplomatic breakthrough, as it occurred during a period when most Western countries, particularly the United States, still recognized **Taiwan** as the legitimate government of China. Trudeau's recognition of the PRC was part of a broader effort to assert Canadian independence in foreign policy and to open new avenues of trade and diplomatic engagement.

Trudeau's decision to engage with China was driven by several factors:

- **Economic interests**: China was seen as a vast and untapped market for Canadian goods, particularly in the agricultural and natural resource sectors.
- **Diplomatic positioning**: Trudeau sought to position Canada as a middle power capable of engaging with both the Eastern and Western blocs during the Cold War, thus enhancing Canada's global influence.
- **Ideological curiosity**: Pierre Trudeau's interest in socialist ideologies and his visits to China contributed to a sense of curiosity and admiration for the Chinese revolution, even if he did not fully endorse its more repressive aspects.

While Trudeau's engagement with China was initially hailed as a diplomatic success, it also raised concerns among some Canadians who feared that the prime minister's relationship with a communist regime would undermine Canada's commitment to democratic values.

Justin Trudeau's Alleged Favoritism Toward Chinese Interests

Justin Trudeau, like his father, has sought to maintain and strengthen Canada's relationship with China. However, his approach has been far more controversial, with allegations of **favoritism** and **over-accommodation** to Chinese interests becoming a persistent theme throughout his time as prime minister. Critics argue that Justin Trudeau has failed to address key issues such as human rights abuses, trade imbalances, and China's growing influence in Canadian politics, leading to concerns that his government is too willing to appease the Chinese Communist Party (CCP).

The "Cash for Access" Scandal

One of the earliest controversies involving Justin Trudeau's relationship with China occurred in 2016, when it was revealed that the Liberal Party had organized a series of exclusive fundraising events attended by wealthy Chinese business figures with ties to the CCP. The so-called **"cash for access" scandal** involved Trudeau attending private fundraising dinners where attendees reportedly paid thousands of dollars for the opportunity to meet the prime minister.

One notable instance involved a fundraising event attended by **Zhang Bin**, a Chinese businessman with connections to the CCP. Shortly after the event, Zhang made a **$1 million donation** to the Pierre Elliott Trudeau Foundation and the University of Montreal, raising concerns that Chinese elites were attempting to buy influence in Canadian politics. Critics argued that the Trudeau government's willingness to accept donations from individuals with close ties to the Chinese government compromised Canada's independence and risked entangling the country in China's influence operations.

Trade and Economic Relations

Under Justin Trudeau, Canada has pursued deeper economic ties with China, with the goal of increasing trade and investment between the two countries. Trudeau's government actively sought a **free trade agreement** with China, and in 2016, he made a high-profile visit to China to promote Canadian businesses and explore opportunities for closer economic cooperation.

However, these efforts have been met with skepticism from both Canadian businesses and political observers, who argue that the Trudeau government has been too eager to secure trade deals at the expense of protecting Canada's economic and strategic interests. Critics have pointed out that China's **state-controlled economy** and its use of **non-market practices** pose significant risks to Canada's industries, particularly in areas like technology and intellectual property. Concerns have also been raised about China's influence over Canadian companies through **state-owned enterprises** (SOEs) and its aggressive approach to acquiring Canadian resources and infrastructure.

Tensions between the two countries reached a breaking point in **2018**, when Canadian authorities arrested **Huawei executive Meng Wanzhou** at the request of the U.S. government. In retaliation, China detained two Canadian citizens, **Michael Kovrig** and **Michael Spavor**, in what was widely seen as an act of **hostage diplomacy**. Despite this, Trudeau's government has been criticized for being slow to take a hard stance against China's actions, with some accusing him of prioritizing economic ties over standing up for Canada's sovereignty and human rights.

Allegations of Chinese Influence in Canadian Elections

In recent years, allegations have surfaced suggesting that China may have attempted to **interfere in Canadian elections** to benefit Justin Trudeau's Liberal Party. In 2021, reports emerged that the **Canadian Security Intelligence Service (CSIS)** had warned the government about Chinese attempts to influence Canadian political candidates. These allegations included claims that Chinese agents had funneled money to certain political campaigns and that pro-China groups had engaged in social media manipulation to sway public opinion in favor of candidates sympathetic to Beijing.

The **Globe and Mail** reported in 2022 that Chinese agents had allegedly funded a network of candidates in the 2019 federal election, with the goal of influencing Canadian foreign policy in a way that would benefit China. While Trudeau has denied any knowledge of such interference, his government has been criticized for not taking a stronger stance against Chinese influence operations in Canada, leading to accusations that he is unwilling to confront China over its actions for fear of damaging economic ties.

Both Pierre and Justin Trudeau have sought to build strong diplomatic and economic ties with China, but their approaches have been shaped by the political contexts of their respective eras. Pierre Trudeau's engagement with China in the 1970s was seen as a bold and strategic move that helped position Canada as an independent actor on the global stage, free from the influence of the United States. However, his son Justin Trudeau's relationship with China has been far more controversial, with accusations of favoritism, economic dependency, and political interference casting a shadow over his government's approach to China.

While Pierre Trudeau's legacy with China is largely remembered as a diplomatic success, Justin Trudeau's handling of Canada-China relations has been marked by scandals, accusations of undue Chinese influence, and tensions over trade and human rights. The Trudeau family's long-standing relationship with China continues to shape Canadian foreign policy, but it has also raised serious questions about the balance between economic engagement and the protection of Canadian sovereignty and democratic values.

Allegations of Foreign Influence on Canadian Policy-Making: Undermining National Sovereignty

In recent years, Canada has faced growing concerns over foreign influence on its policy-making processes, raising fears that external actors, particularly foreign governments and corporations, are undermining the country's national sovereignty. Allegations of foreign interference have primarily involved **China**, but other actors, such as **Saudi Arabia**, **Russia**, and **corporate interests**, have also been implicated. These accusations suggest that foreign influence is shaping Canadian domestic and foreign policy in ways that prioritize the interests of external powers over the well-being and sovereignty of Canada.

The most prominent allegations revolve around interference in **Canadian elections**, **trade agreements**, **environmental policies**, and **strategic infrastructure projects**, raising questions about the integrity of Canada's political system and its ability to defend its national interests in a globalized world.

Chinese Influence: Political Interference and Economic Leverage

China has been at the center of many of the allegations regarding foreign influence in Canada, particularly under the leadership of **Justin Trudeau**. There are accusations that the Chinese Communist Party (CCP) has used **economic leverage**, **political donations**, and **interference in democratic processes** to advance its interests within Canada.

Allegations of Chinese Election Interference

One of the most significant concerns surrounding Chinese influence in Canada involves allegations of interference in Canadian federal elections. In 2021, **Canadian Security Intelligence Service (CSIS)** reports warned that China had attempted to influence the 2019 federal election by supporting specific political candidates deemed favorable to Chinese interests. According to reports, Chinese agents allegedly funded certain candidates and used social media manipulation to sway public opinion. The goal of this alleged interference was to secure a more **pro-China foreign policy** from Canada and protect Chinese interests within the country.

The **Globe and Mail** reported that Chinese agents had targeted specific ridings in the 2019 election, directing funds and resources toward candidates who would be sympathetic to Beijing's objectives. This raised concerns about the integrity of Canada's democratic process, as foreign actors sought to influence the outcome of elections in a way that could shift national policies in China's favor.

Despite these alarming reports, critics argue that the **Trudeau government** has been reluctant to take strong action against Chinese interference, possibly due to the significant economic ties between Canada and China. This reluctance has led to accusations that the government is failing to adequately protect Canadian sovereignty from external interference.

Economic Influence and Corporate Ties

China's influence on Canadian policy-making has also been linked to its **economic leverage** over Canadian businesses and politicians. Over the past decade, China has become an increasingly important trading partner for Canada, particularly in sectors like **natural resources**, **agriculture**, and **technology**. However, this growing economic relationship has led to concerns that Canada's trade policies and national security are being compromised in exchange for economic benefits.

A prominent example of this dynamic was the controversy surrounding **Huawei** and its potential involvement in Canada's **5G telecommunications infrastructure**. Huawei, a Chinese technology company with close ties to the CCP, was seen as a potential security threat by many Canadian allies, including the United States. Despite these concerns, Trudeau's government initially hesitated to block Huawei from participating in Canada's 5G network, sparking allegations that the government was prioritizing economic relations with China over national security.

Similarly, the 2016 **cash-for-access scandal** highlighted concerns about China's influence on Canadian political figures. The scandal involved Liberal Party fundraising events attended by wealthy Chinese businesspeople with close ties to the CCP. These events raised questions about the extent to which Chinese interests were influencing Canadian politicians through donations and private meetings. One high-profile case involved a **$1 million donation** to the **Pierre Elliott Trudeau Foundation** by a Chinese billionaire, which many viewed as an attempt to curry favor with the Trudeau government.

Saudi Arabian and Russian Influence: Strategic Interests and Soft Power

While China has received the most attention regarding allegations of foreign influence in Canada, other countries such as **Saudi Arabia** and **Russia** have also been implicated in attempts to shape Canadian policy to suit their interests.

Saudi Arabian Influence and Foreign Policy

Saudi Arabia has used its **economic ties** and **diplomatic pressure** to influence Canada's foreign policy decisions. The most notable example occurred in **2018**, when Saudi Arabia responded to Canadian criticism of its human rights record by initiating a **diplomatic and economic crisis**. Canada's foreign minister at the time, **Chrystia Freeland**, had called for the release of imprisoned Saudi activists, including **Raif Badawi** and his sister. In retaliation, Saudi Arabia expelled the Canadian ambassador, froze trade, and recalled Saudi students studying in Canada.

This incident raised concerns about the extent to which foreign governments could retaliate against Canada for criticizing their domestic policies. The Saudi government's aggressive response sent a message that economic and diplomatic pressure could be used to silence Canadian criticism, especially regarding human rights. This has had a chilling effect on Canada's willingness to confront authoritarian regimes, as there are concerns about the economic fallout that could result from taking a strong stance on human rights.

Russian Influence: Disinformation and Cybersecurity Threats

Russia's influence on Canadian policy has been more subtle but no less significant, primarily through its use of **disinformation campaigns** and **cyberattacks**. Like other Western democracies, Canada has been the target of **Russian disinformation** efforts designed to sow discord and undermine trust in democratic institutions. Russia has also been implicated in **cyberattacks** against Canadian government institutions and businesses, which threaten national security and economic stability.

In 2017, **CSIS** issued a report warning that Russian disinformation campaigns were attempting to influence Canadian public opinion on key issues, including Canada's involvement in **NATO** and its stance on **Ukraine**. These campaigns typically involve the spread of **false information** on social media and other platforms to shape public opinion and weaken support for Canada's foreign policy initiatives.

Corporate Interests and Environmental Policy

In addition to foreign governments, **corporate interests**—particularly multinational corporations—have also been accused of exerting undue influence on Canadian policy-making. This is especially evident in the realm of **environmental policy**, where oil and gas companies, as well as foreign investors, have lobbied aggressively against regulations aimed at curbing climate change.

Critics argue that these corporate interests, including **foreign-owned oil companies**, have used their economic clout to pressure the Canadian government into adopting more industry-friendly policies. For example, the decision to approve certain pipeline projects, despite significant opposition from environmental groups and Indigenous communities, has been seen as evidence of foreign corporate influence on Canadian environmental policy. This has led to concerns that Canada's sovereignty is being compromised by external economic interests, particularly in industries that have global investors with vested interests in shaping domestic policy.

Allegations of foreign influence in Canadian policy-making have raised serious concerns about the country's ability to defend its national interests in an increasingly globalized world. From China's political and economic leverage to Saudi Arabia's diplomatic pressure and Russia's disinformation campaigns, Canada faces significant challenges in maintaining its sovereignty in the face of foreign interference.

While Canada's open and democratic political system makes it vulnerable to external influence, critics argue that the government has not done enough to protect the integrity of its institutions and policies. The Trudeau government, in particular, has been accused of being overly accommodating to foreign powers such as China, raising fears that economic and political interests are being prioritized over the defense of Canadian sovereignty and democratic values.

Conclusion: The Fall of the Trudeau Dynasty

A Legacy of Corruption and Division

Summing Up the Long-Lasting Damage Caused by Two Generations of Trudeau Leadership

The Trudeau family, both Pierre and Justin, has undeniably left an indelible mark on Canada. While they are credited with many achievements in diplomacy, social reform, and nation-building, they have also been criticized for causing long-lasting harm to various aspects of Canadian society, governance, and identity. Both leaders pursued bold, often controversial, policies that reshaped the political, cultural, and economic landscape of Canada, with effects that are still being debated today.

Pierre Trudeau: The Architect of National Division

1. National Energy Program (NEP):
   One of Pierre Trudeau's most criticized policies, the NEP was designed to increase Canadian control over the country's energy resources and ensure energy self-sufficiency. However, it disproportionately targeted Alberta and Western Canada's oil wealth, leading to economic turmoil in the region. The NEP is often cited as the beginning of Western alienation, where many Western Canadians felt exploited by central Canada. This

economic divide fueled regional resentment that persists to this day.

2. **Multiculturalism Policy:**
   While the official Multiculturalism Policy introduced by Pierre Trudeau in 1971 was hailed as a progressive move to accommodate Canada's diverse population, critics argue that it contributed to the fragmentation of Canadian identity. By promoting the celebration of individual ethnic cultures over a cohesive national identity, some believe it weakened traditional values and undermined Canada's core institutions, leading to a more fragmented and less unified country.

3. **The War Measures Act during the October Crisis:**
   Pierre Trudeau's invocation of the War Measures Act during the 1970 October Crisis in response to the FLQ kidnappings in Quebec was seen by many as an overreach of government power. The suspension of civil liberties across Canada and the mass arrests without due process led to deep mistrust of the government and concern about the state's authoritarian tendencies, marking a significant moment in Canada's democratic history.

Justin Trudeau: Continuation and Expansion of Controversial Policies

1. **Economic and Energy Policies:**
   Justin Trudeau has been heavily criticized for his carbon tax and environmental policies, which many in the oil-rich provinces of Alberta and Saskatchewan view as further economic marginalization. His cancellation of critical pipeline projects, such as Northern Gateway and Energy East, coupled with the push for a transition away from fossil fuels, has led to continued Western alienation. Many Western Canadians believe that their economic livelihoods are being sacrificed for the political and environmental goals of urban, eastern Canada.
2. **Perceived Favoritism Toward Eastern Canada:**
   Like his father, Justin Trudeau has been accused of favoring central and eastern Canada, particularly Quebec, over the interests of Western provinces. This sense of favoritism, alongside allegations of corporate cronyism in Quebec-based companies like SNC-Lavalin, has eroded trust in the federal government in the West.
3. **Cultural Fragmentation and "Post-National" Vision:**
   Justin Trudeau's "post-national" vision of Canada, in which he famously declared that Canada has "no core identity," has further contributed to the erosion of a cohesive Canadian culture. His government's policies, which promote multiculturalism, immigration,

and diversity over the preservation of traditional Canadian values, have led to cultural fragmentation. Critics argue that this approach weakens national unity, particularly in rural and conservative areas of the country, where traditional values are still deeply held.

4. Ethics and Scandals:
   Justin Trudeau's leadership has been marred by several high-profile ethics scandals, including the SNC-Lavalin affair and the WE Charity scandal. These incidents have raised questions about transparency, ethics in governance, and whether Trudeau's government is unduly influenced by corporate elites and foreign actors, particularly China. These scandals have damaged public trust in Canadian institutions and eroded confidence in the government's ability to act in the best interests of its citizens.

The Damage to National Unity and Sovereignty

1. Western Alienation and Separatist Movements:
   The policies of both Pierre and Justin Trudeau have significantly contributed to Western alienation, a sense of political and economic exclusion felt by the western provinces. This alienation has given rise to separatist movements such as Wexit, which advocates for the separation of Western Canada from the rest of the country. The

growing support for such movements is a clear indication of the long-term damage caused by the Trudeau governments' policies, which have deepened regional divides and undermined national unity.

2. Quebec's Sovereignty Movement: Pierre Trudeau's attempts to address Quebec's aspirations for independence were largely seen as unsuccessful, with the province's sovereignty movement peaking in the 1980s and 1990s. Justin Trudeau has largely ignored the issue, focusing instead on fostering Quebec's economic development. However, the tensions between federalism and Quebec's unique cultural identity remain unresolved, creating an ongoing challenge to Canada's national unity.

3. Foreign Influence and Loss of Sovereignty: Both Trudeau governments have been accused of compromising Canadian sovereignty. Pierre Trudeau's admiration for socialist regimes and non-aligned countries led to concerns about Canada's role in global geopolitics during the Cold War. Justin Trudeau's alleged favoritism toward Chinese interests, the cash-for-access scandal, and allegations of foreign interference in Canadian elections have further eroded public trust in the government's ability to defend Canada's sovereignty against external influences.

Can Canada Recover from the Corruption, Economic Damage, and Social Fragmentation Left by the Trudeau Legacy?

The legacies of both Pierre and Justin Trudeau have reshaped Canada in profound and lasting ways, leaving behind deep divisions, economic challenges, and allegations of corruption that continue to impact the country today. As Canadians reflect on the political, economic, and social changes brought about by two generations of Trudeau leadership, the question arises: Can Canada recover from the damage caused by the Trudeau era? To answer this, it's essential to examine the key areas affected: corruption and public trust, economic damage and energy sector challenges, and social fragmentation and regional divisions.

1. Corruption and Public Trust: Rebuilding Institutional Integrity

Both Trudeau administrations have been marred by ethical scandals that have damaged public trust in government institutions. Pierre Trudeau's time in office was characterized by authoritarian measures such as invoking the War Measures Act during the October Crisis, which many viewed as an overreach of government power. Justin Trudeau's leadership has been similarly tainted by multiple high-profile scandals, including the SNC-Lavalin affair and the WE Charity controversy. These incidents have raised serious concerns about transparency, accountability, and the undue influence of corporate elites and foreign actors—particularly China—on Canadian policy-making.

Can Public Trust Be Restored?

Recovering from the erosion of public trust will require a concerted effort by future Canadian governments to prioritize ethics reform, greater transparency, and accountability. This could include:

- **Stronger ethics laws:** Enacting stricter rules to limit the influence of corporate donations, lobbying, and foreign influence on Canadian politics.
- **Independent investigations:** Ensuring that investigations into government corruption are handled by independent bodies with the authority to hold political leaders accountable.
- **Transparency in governance:** Encouraging open government practices, such as publishing lobbying activities, government contracts, and the decision-making process.

Restoring faith in Canada's institutions will be a long process, but it is crucial for maintaining a healthy democracy. If the country's leaders can take meaningful action to address these issues, public confidence in government may slowly be rebuilt.

2. Economic Damage and Energy Sector Challenges: Rebuilding Canada's Economic Future

Canada's economy has faced significant challenges under both Trudeau administrations, particularly in Western Canada. Pierre Trudeau's National Energy Program (NEP) caused deep economic damage in Alberta and other western provinces, where it was seen as an attempt by the federal government to centralize control of the country's energy resources. Justin Trudeau's carbon tax, environmental regulations, and pipeline cancellations have similarly been viewed as hostile to the oil and gas sector, exacerbating economic hardships in the West.

Can Canada Recover Economically?

While the Canadian economy is resilient, it will take significant effort to recover from the economic damage caused by these policies. Some steps that could help include:

- Reinvigorating the energy sector: Supporting the development of energy infrastructure, including oil and gas pipelines, while balancing environmental concerns. Canada's natural resources remain a crucial part of its economy, and a pragmatic approach to energy policy is essential for economic recovery, particularly in Alberta and Saskatchewan.
- Diversifying the economy: In addition to bolstering traditional industries, Canada should invest in innovation, technology, and renewable energy sectors to create new growth

opportunities and reduce reliance on volatile global markets.

- Reforming tax policies: Revisiting policies such as the carbon tax to ensure they are not disproportionately burdening key sectors of the economy, particularly resource-heavy industries in the West.

Economic recovery is possible, but it will require addressing the grievances of Western provinces and implementing policies that balance environmental stewardship with economic growth. A more collaborative approach between provincial and federal governments is essential to this recovery.

3. Social Fragmentation and Regional Divides: Healing a Fractured Nation

One of the most significant long-term effects of the Trudeau leadership has been the deepening of social fragmentation and regional divisions. Pierre Trudeau's policies, particularly the NEP, gave rise to Western alienation, which was further fueled by Justin Trudeau's progressive social policies and environmental agenda. Meanwhile, the promotion of multiculturalism has been criticized for eroding a sense of shared national identity, as Justin Trudeau's post-national vision has shifted the focus away from traditional Canadian values.

Can Canada Heal Its Social Divides?

Healing Canada's fractured social landscape will require leadership that prioritizes national unity while respecting the diversity of regional interests. Steps toward achieving this include:

- Balancing regional interests: Future governments must make a concerted effort to address the concerns of Western Canada, including offering more control over natural resources and ensuring that policies don't disproportionately harm specific regions. A restructured federalism that offers greater provincial autonomy might help reduce the tensions caused by centralized decision-making.
- Strengthening national identity: While multiculturalism remains a core Canadian value, there needs to be a balance between celebrating diversity and fostering a unifying sense of national identity. This could involve promoting civic engagement, shared values, and national symbols that bring Canadians together, rather than focusing solely on diversity.
- Addressing rural-urban divides: The divide between urban and rural Canada has grown more pronounced in recent years, particularly as progressive policies from urban centers clash with more conservative values in rural areas. Bridging this gap will require addressing the economic and cultural

concerns of rural Canadians and ensuring that their voices are heard in the political process.

While these social divides run deep, they are not insurmountable. With the right leadership and a focus on inclusivity that respects both diversity and national unity, Canada can begin to heal its social fragmentation.

Looking Ahead: Is the Trudeau Era Truly Over, or Will Their Legacy Continue to Shape Canada's Political Landscape?

As Canada stands at a political crossroads, the question of whether the Trudeau era is truly over or whether its legacy will continue to influence the country's future remains a pressing issue. Both Pierre and Justin Trudeau left a profound mark on Canadian politics, culture, and society, and while their leadership may no longer dominate the political stage in the same way, the policies, ideologies, and divisions they fostered are likely to have lasting implications for the country.

1. End of the Trudeau Era: A Possible Turning Point

With Justin Trudeau's popularity waning in recent years due to multiple scandals, economic challenges, and growing regional dissatisfaction, there is a growing sentiment among some Canadians that the Trudeau era is coming to an end. Justin Trudeau's leadership has been marred by significant controversies such as the SNC-Lavalin affair, WE Charity scandal, and allegations of foreign influence in Canadian policy-making. His progressive social policies and environmental regulations have alienated large swaths of Western Canada, fueling separatist movements like Wexit.

If Justin Trudeau were to step down or lose in future elections, it would mark the end of an era where the Trudeau name held significant sway over Canadian politics. A shift in leadership, particularly if the Conservative Party or another political force were to rise, could signal a departure from the progressive and multiculturalist policies that have defined the Trudeau legacy. This change would likely bring with it new priorities, such as a stronger focus on national unity, economic recovery, and Western concerns, while possibly reversing or moderating some of the more divisive Trudeau-era policies.

However, while a change in leadership may signal the end of the Trudeau name in power, the broader political and social forces unleashed by both Pierre and Justin Trudeau may be far more enduring.

2. The Continuing Influence of the Trudeau Legacy: Policy and Ideological Shifts

While the Trudeau family may no longer dominate the political stage after Justin, the legacy of their policies and ideologies will likely continue to shape Canadian politics for decades to come. Both Pierre and Justin Trudeau left behind deep ideological frameworks that have become embedded in the Canadian political system and will be difficult to dismantle.

Multiculturalism and Progressive Values

One of the most lasting impacts of the Trudeau legacy has been the normalization of multiculturalism as a central tenet of Canadian identity. Pierre Trudeau introduced official multiculturalism in 1971, and this has since become a defining feature of Canada's global image. Justin Trudeau has expanded on this, embracing a post-national vision of Canada that emphasizes inclusivity, diversity, and progressive social values. Even if a future government adopts a more conservative platform, it is unlikely that these policies will be entirely reversed.

Canada's commitment to multiculturalism, immigration, and diversity has become deeply ingrained in its political culture, and subsequent governments are likely to continue to promote these values, albeit perhaps with a different emphasis. The debate may shift from whether multiculturalism should be a core part of Canadian identity to how it should be managed to foster greater national unity and cohesion, particularly in light of growing social fragmentation and regional divides.

Environmental and Social Policies

Justin Trudeau's progressive social policies, including those related to gender identity, LGBTQ+ rights, Indigenous reconciliation, and climate change, have defined his tenure. These issues are not likely to disappear from the political discourse, even after Trudeau's departure. Future governments may modify or recalibrate these policies, but the fundamental emphasis on social progressivism will continue to shape debates in Canada. Climate change, for example, has become a defining issue of the 21st century, and Canada's approach to balancing environmental concerns with economic growth is a debate that will endure.

Moreover, the carbon tax, introduced by Justin Trudeau's government, will likely remain a contentious issue in Canadian politics. While some regions of Canada, particularly in the West, view the carbon tax as damaging to the economy, others see it as an essential tool in the fight against climate change. The political debate over how Canada should address its environmental responsibilities will continue to be shaped by the policies and precedents set during the Trudeau era.

3. Social Fragmentation and Regional Divides: A Continuing Challenge

The Trudeau legacy has deepened social fragmentation and regional divides in Canada. Both Pierre and Justin Trudeau are viewed in Western Canada as centralizing power in Ottawa at the expense of the West's economic and political autonomy. The National Energy Program (NEP) under Pierre Trudeau and Justin Trudeau's carbon tax and pipeline policies have fueled Western alienation and given rise to movements like Wexit. Even if a new government emerges, addressing these long-standing grievances will remain a challenge.

Western Canada's sense of alienation from the federal government, especially in Alberta and Saskatchewan, has grown stronger in recent years. The failure to meaningfully address the West's concerns over energy, resource management, and regional representation could keep the issue of separatism on the political agenda. If future governments fail to reconcile these divides, Canada's political landscape will remain fractured.

Quebec, too, continues to have a complicated relationship with the federal government. The Quebec sovereignty movement has quieted in recent years, but the province's desire to maintain its cultural and political autonomy remains strong. Justin Trudeau's policies have largely placated Quebec by emphasizing economic benefits and autonomy within the framework of the federal system, but tensions could resurface if future governments neglect Quebec's unique position in Canadian politics.

4. The Next Generation of Canadian Leadership: A New Era or Continuation of Trudeauism?

The Trudeau name has become synonymous with progressivism, multiculturalism, and centralized governance. As Justin Trudeau faces increased opposition and growing calls for change, the next generation of Canadian leadership—whether conservative, centrist, or even more progressive—will need to navigate the political landscape shaped by the Trudeau family.

The Conservative Party of Canada and other political forces could present a more decentralized approach to governance, focusing on provincial autonomy, economic growth, and traditional values. However, they will need to do so in a country that has been deeply influenced by Trudeau-era values such as diversity, inclusivity, and social progressivism. Whether they choose to dismantle or moderate these policies, the next generation of leaders will still be operating within the context of a country that has been profoundly shaped by the Trudeau legacy.

While the Trudeau family may not dominate Canadian politics forever, their policies, ideologies, and impact on the country's identity and political landscape are likely to endure for the foreseeable future. Even if Justin Trudeau steps down or loses power, the progressive social policies, multiculturalism, and environmental agendas that define the Trudeau legacy are now deeply embedded in Canadian politics. These issues will continue to influence public debate and future governments, regardless of who takes power next.

Canada's ability to move forward will depend on how future leaders address the regional divides, social fragmentation, and economic challenges that have been exacerbated during the Trudeau years. Whether the Trudeau era is truly over or simply transitioning to a new phase of Canadian politics remains to be seen, but its influence will undoubtedly be felt for years to come

Epilogue: The Path to Reform

Steps Needed for Canada to Break Free from the Trudeau Dynasty's Lingering Influence

The **Trudeau dynasty**, spanning over five decades with the leadership of **Pierre** and **Justin Trudeau**, has left a deep and lasting imprint on Canada's political, cultural, and economic fabric. While the Trudeau name has been associated with progressive policies, multiculturalism, and a centralized governance model, many Canadians feel that it has also led to **regional alienation**, **economic challenges**, and **social fragmentation**. For Canada to move forward and break free from the lingering influence of the Trudeau dynasty, a set of decisive steps must be taken to address the underlying issues created during their leadership. These steps include reforming **national unity**, **political decentralization**, **economic revitalization**, and fostering a new national identity.

1. Political Decentralization: Empowering the Provinces

One of the most enduring criticisms of both Pierre and Justin Trudeau has been their emphasis on **centralized governance**, often to the detriment of provincial autonomy. Pierre Trudeau's **National Energy Program (NEP)** and Justin Trudeau's **carbon tax** and **pipeline cancellations** have alienated provinces, particularly in **Western Canada**. To break free from the Trudeau model of governance, Canada must decentralize political power, allowing provinces greater control over their resources and decision-making.

Steps toward decentralization:

- **Greater provincial control over natural resources**: Western provinces, especially **Alberta** and **Saskatchewan**, have long called for more autonomy in managing their natural resources. Allowing provinces to regulate their own energy sectors could foster regional economic growth while addressing long-standing grievances.
- **Reforming the federalism model**: Shifting toward a more collaborative federal model where provinces have increased decision-making power in areas such as healthcare, education, and environmental policy could reduce the dominance of Ottawa in national politics. This would help address the deep **regional divides** that have been exacerbated under the Trudeau leadership.

Decentralization could help heal the **alienation** felt by Western provinces and other regions, fostering a sense of **ownership** and engagement with the political process.

2. Restoring National Unity: Addressing Regional and Social Divides

The Trudeau legacy has left Canada with deep regional and social divisions, particularly between **Western**

Canada, **Quebec**, and the rest of the country. Western alienation, sparked by Pierre Trudeau's **National Energy Program** and exacerbated by Justin Trudeau's **environmental policies**, has led to movements like **Wexit** that advocate for Western independence. Quebec's relationship with the federal government has similarly remained fraught with **sovereignty tensions**.

Steps to restore unity:

- **National reconciliation strategy**: A government committed to national unity must develop a **reconciliation plan** to address the specific grievances of **Western Canada** and **Quebec**. This strategy should include economic policies that benefit all regions of the country and acknowledge the unique contributions of each province.
- **Regional representation in government**: Ensuring that all provinces have a fair say in national decision-making through reforms to the **Senate** or by enhancing **regional representation** in the **House of Commons** could reduce the perception that certain provinces are being ignored by the federal government.
- **Open dialogue on separatist movements**: Rather than dismissing separatist movements like **Wexit** or Quebec's **sovereignty movement**, the federal government should engage in dialogue with these groups. Addressing their concerns head-on could prevent these movements from gaining further momentum.

By fostering **national dialogue** and emphasizing cooperation between regions, Canada can move away from the **division** and **fragmentation** that have characterized the Trudeau era.

3. Economic Revitalization: Supporting Growth Beyond Resource Dependency

Both Pierre and Justin Trudeau's economic policies have been criticized for exacerbating **regional economic disparities**, particularly in resource-rich areas like Alberta. The **carbon tax** and cancellation of key energy infrastructure projects have hurt Western Canada's economy, while corporate favoritism scandals such as the **SNC-Lavalin affair** have raised questions about the integrity of Canadian economic policy.

Steps to revitalize the economy:

- **Balancing environmental goals with economic growth**: While climate change and environmental sustainability must remain a priority, economic policies that unfairly target the energy sector or resource-dependent provinces can create more harm than good. Canada must strike a balance between **reducing carbon emissions** and fostering **economic growth** in all regions, particularly by investing in technologies that help the energy sector transition without job losses.
- **Supporting regional industries**: Economic diversification is key to reducing dependency on

the energy sector. Investments in **technology, innovation, renewable energy**, and **manufacturing** can help provinces like Alberta and Saskatchewan expand their economic base. Additionally, investments in **infrastructure** and **regional development** programs can spur economic growth across Canada, not just in the urban centers of central and eastern Canada.

- **Corporate accountability**: Implementing stricter regulations on corporate lobbying and political donations could prevent undue influence by corporate interests, as seen in the SNC-Lavalin affair. This would ensure that Canada's economic policies serve the **public interest**, not just a select few.

4. Rebuilding Public Trust and Accountability: Addressing Corruption

Both Trudeau administrations have been plagued by **scandals** and allegations of **corruption**, with **cash-for-access** fundraisers, the **WE Charity scandal**, and the **SNC-Lavalin affair** undermining public confidence in government. A clear path forward for Canada involves **restoring public trust** and ensuring that politicians are held accountable for ethical lapses.

Steps to rebuild trust:

- **Ethics reform**: Strengthening **ethics rules** for politicians, banning **corporate donations**, and limiting **lobbyist influence** in political decision-making are crucial to restoring public faith in governance. Additionally, ensuring that the **Ethics Commissioner** and other oversight bodies have real enforcement powers would provide more effective oversight.

- **Transparency initiatives**: Implementing more stringent transparency measures in government, such as **public reporting of donations**, **lobbyist activities**, and **political contracts**, would ensure that the public has full visibility into how decisions are made.
- **Independent investigations**: Establishing truly independent bodies that can investigate political misconduct and issue penalties would help deter future ethical violations.

Transparency and accountability are key to rebuilding **institutional integrity** and ensuring that future governments prioritize the **public good** over personal or corporate interests.

5. Fostering a New National Identity: Moving Beyond the Trudeau Legacy

One of the most challenging aspects of moving beyond the Trudeau era will be redefining **Canadian identity**. Both Pierre and Justin Trudeau promoted **multiculturalism** and **progressive social policies**, but critics argue that their vision of a **post-national** Canada, where there is "no core identity," has created social fragmentation. For Canada to move forward, it will need to foster a **unified national identity** that respects diversity while also emphasizing shared values and traditions.

Steps to foster a new identity:

- **Promoting national unity through shared values**: While **multiculturalism** should remain a core Canadian value, the country must also prioritize a sense of **shared purpose**. National unity can be promoted by focusing on civic engagement, **patriotism**, and **national pride**, while acknowledging the contributions of diverse communities.
- **Emphasizing Canadian heritage**: Canada's rich history and cultural heritage should be celebrated, alongside the promotion of diversity. By balancing respect for traditional values with inclusivity, Canada can create a national identity that unites all Canadians.
- **Building a forward-looking national narrative**: Canada's identity should not solely be rooted in the past but should also be focused on the future. Emphasizing **innovation, global leadership**, and **civic responsibility** as key elements of Canadian identity will inspire future generations to take pride in their country.

Proposals for Reform in Governance, Economy, and Civil Liberties to Undo the Damage Caused Over Decades

Over the course of multiple Trudeau-led administrations, Canada has experienced significant political, economic, and social changes. While some reforms brought progress, critics argue that the legacy left behind has also caused **economic stagnation**, **regional alienation**, and the **erosion of civil liberties**. To address these issues and move Canada forward, a comprehensive approach to **reform in governance, the economy, and civil liberties** is necessary. Below are proposals aimed at undoing the damage caused over decades and fostering a more prosperous, united, and free Canada.

1. Governance Reforms: Enhancing Accountability and Decentralization

To address **corruption**, **centralized power**, and the **marginalization of regions**, governance reforms should focus on enhancing **accountability**, **decentralizing power**, and promoting **regional representation**.

A. Strengthening Ethical Standards and Accountability

Public trust in government has eroded due to numerous scandals, including **SNC-Lavalin**, **WE Charity**, and the **cash-for-access** controversies. To restore faith in institutions, Canada needs robust reforms to combat corruption and increase accountability in politics.

Proposals:

- **Independent Ethics Oversight**: Strengthen the role of the **Ethics Commissioner** by granting them full investigative powers and ensuring true independence from the government. This would include making the commissioner's decisions legally binding and expanding their remit to oversee all senior officials.
- **Ban on Corporate and Foreign Donations**: Implement a comprehensive ban on **corporate donations** and any political contributions from **foreign entities** to reduce undue influence in policymaking. This would help prevent scandals like those involving foreign donors with ties to China.
- **Transparency in Lobbying**: Enforce stricter transparency laws on lobbying activities, including mandatory public disclosure of all meetings between lobbyists and government officials. This would ensure that citizens are aware of external influences on government policies.
- **Mandatory Conflict-of-Interest Disclosures**: Require politicians to publicly disclose all **potential conflicts of interest** before taking office, including business ties and financial interests that could influence decision-making.

B. Decentralization of Power: Empowering Provincial Governments

The long-standing practice of **centralized governance** in Ottawa has alienated many regions, particularly

Western Canada. Decentralizing power by giving more autonomy to provinces would foster national unity, reduce tensions, and allow regional governments to address the specific needs of their populations.

Proposals:

- **Provincial Control over Natural Resources**: Transfer more authority over natural resources, including oil, gas, and mining, to the provinces. This would ensure that provinces like Alberta and Saskatchewan have greater control over their economies and reduce the sense of **Western alienation**.
- **Strengthening the Role of Provinces in National Policy**: Implement a system where provinces have a stronger voice in national policymaking, especially on issues that disproportionately affect them, such as environmental regulations, energy policy, and healthcare. An enhanced **Council of the Federation** could serve as a platform for provincial leaders to engage directly with federal decision-makers.
- **Senate Reform**: Transform the **Canadian Senate** into a more representative body, potentially adopting a model where provinces appoint or elect senators to better represent regional interests, ensuring that all areas of the country have fair input in national decisions.

2. Economic Reforms: Fostering Growth and Reducing Dependence

Decades of economic policies that stifle the energy sector, increase taxation, and prioritize central Canadian interests over resource-rich regions have left Canada divided and economically stagnant. To rejuvenate the economy, reforms should focus on **supporting resource industries**, **diversifying the economy**, and **reducing taxation** to encourage investment and innovation.

A. Reviving the Energy Sector

Canada's **oil and gas industry**, particularly in **Western Canada**, has faced significant challenges due to policies such as the **carbon tax** and the cancellation of key pipeline projects. Revitalizing this sector is crucial for economic recovery and regional prosperity.

Proposals:

- **Pipeline Approvals and Energy Infrastructure**: Accelerate the approval and construction of key **energy infrastructure projects**, including oil pipelines and liquefied natural gas (LNG) terminals. Ensuring safe and environmentally responsible pipeline development will help Canada expand energy exports and create jobs in resource-rich provinces.
- **Balanced Environmental Policies**: Reevaluate environmental regulations, such as the carbon

tax, to strike a balance between **environmental sustainability** and **economic growth**. Provinces should have more flexibility in meeting national climate goals based on their unique economic conditions, allowing for energy sector growth alongside environmental protection efforts.

- **Investment in Renewable Energy**: Encourage investment in **renewable energy projects**, such as solar, wind, and hydroelectric power, particularly in provinces looking to diversify their economies. These initiatives would reduce dependence on traditional energy sources while preparing Canada for the energy transition.

B. Reducing Tax Burdens and Encouraging Investment

High tax rates, particularly corporate taxes, have stifled economic growth and discouraged investment. By reducing tax burdens and supporting innovation, Canada can foster a more competitive and dynamic economy.

Proposals:

- **Corporate Tax Reform**: Lower the **corporate tax rate** to make Canada more attractive to international businesses and encourage domestic companies to expand. By creating a favorable tax environment, Canada can become a hub for innovation and entrepreneurship.
- **Tax Incentives for Innovation**: Introduce **tax incentives** for companies investing in **research**

and development, **technology**, and **renewable energy projects**. These incentives would spur innovation and help diversify Canada's economy, especially in industries beyond oil and gas.

- **Support for Small and Medium-Sized Enterprises (SMEs)**: Implement policies that support **SMEs**, including reducing bureaucratic red tape, offering low-interest loans, and providing tax breaks for new businesses. SMEs are the backbone of the Canadian economy, and fostering their growth will create jobs and boost the economy.

3. Civil Liberties and Rights: Strengthening Protections and Reducing Government Overreach

The **Trudeau administrations**, both under Pierre and Justin, have been criticized for overreaching government powers, particularly with the invocation of the **War Measures Act** during the October Crisis and more recently, with **restrictions on civil liberties** during the COVID-19 pandemic. To restore civil liberties and prevent future government overreach, reforms must ensure stronger protections for individual freedoms and accountability in emergency measures.

A. Protecting Freedom of Speech and Expression

Recent trends in **censorship**, particularly with regard to **online content** and restrictions on free speech, have raised concerns about the state of civil liberties in Canada. Strengthening protections for freedom of expression is critical to preserving Canada's democratic values.

Proposals:

- **Amending Bill C-10 and Bill C-36**: These controversial bills, which seek to regulate online content and combat hate speech, have been criticized for their potential to infringe on free expression. Amending or repealing these laws to ensure they do not restrict legitimate free speech or give excessive power to government regulators will be key in safeguarding civil liberties.
- **Strengthening Freedom of the Press**: Implement clearer legal protections for **journalists** and **whistleblowers** to ensure they can hold the government and corporations accountable without fear of retribution. Canada's democracy relies on a free and independent press to challenge power.

B. Limiting Government Overreach During Crises

Both Pierre and Justin Trudeau's governments have used **emergency powers** to infringe on civil liberties—whether through the War Measures Act or pandemic-related lockdowns. Creating safeguards that limit the government's ability to restrict freedoms is essential to maintaining a democratic society.

Proposals:

- **Review of Emergency Powers**: Conduct a thorough review of the federal government's use of emergency powers and ensure that any future invocation of these powers is **time-limited** and subject to parliamentary oversight.
- **Enshrining Civil Liberties in Law**: Strengthen legal protections for civil liberties, including freedom of assembly, movement, and speech, to prevent future governments from overstepping their bounds under the guise of national emergencies.

Canada faces significant challenges due to decades of **centralized governance**, **economic mismanagement**, and **eroded civil liberties**. However, through targeted reforms in **governance, economy,** and **civil liberties**, the country can recover from these damages and build a stronger, more united future. By decentralizing power, fostering economic growth, and ensuring robust protections for individual freedoms, Canada can move beyond the legacies of past administrations and create a more prosperous and equitable society for all Canadians.

APPENIX

SOURCES

- **The Canadian Encyclopedia: The Trudeau Family**

https://www.thecanadianencyclopedia.ca/en/articl e/trudeau-family

- **Maclean's: The Political Legacy of the Trudeau Family**
  https://www.macleans.ca/politics/the-political-legacy-of-the-trudeau-family/
- **CBC News: Trudeau Family in Canadian Politics**
  https://www.cbc.ca/news/politics/trudeau-family-legacy-in-canadian-politics-1.3290365
- **The Guardian: The Trudeau Brand**
  https://www.theguardian.com/world/2015/sep/21/ justin-trudeau-canada-liberal-party-prime-minister
- **National Post: Pierre Trudeau's Legacy**
  https://nationalpost.com/news/canada/pierre-trudeaus-legacy
- **Maclean's: Justin Trudeau and the Charisma Factor**
  https://www.macleans.ca/politics/justin-trudeau-and-the-power-of-charisma/
- **The Canadian Encyclopedia: Pierre Trudeau's Impact on Canada**
  https://www.thecanadianencyclopedia.ca/en/articl e/pierre-elliott-trudeau
- **The Globe and Mail: Justin Trudeau's Political Legacy**
  https://www.theglobeandmail.com/opinion/editor ials/article-justin-trudeau-the-legacy-of-the-second-trudeau/
- **The New York Times: The Trudeau Family and Canadian Politics**

https://www.nytimes.com/2021/04/22/world/cana
da/trudeau-family-politics.html

4. Exploring Pierre's Background, Education, and His Early Sympathies with Communist Ideologies

- **The Guardian: Pierre Trudeau's Early Life and Ideologies**
  https://www.theguardian.com/world/2017/oct/03/
  pierre-trudeau-early-life-education-politics
- **CBC News: Pierre Trudeau and Communist Ideologies**
  https://www.cbc.ca/news/canada/pierre-trudeau-communist-sympathies-1.4299028
- **The Canadian Encyclopedia: Pierre Trudeau and His Political Ideas**
  https://www.thecanadianencyclopedia.ca/en/articl
  e/pierre-elliott-trudeau

5. How His Intellectual Leanings Influenced His Political Decisions

- **The Globe and Mail: Pierre Trudeau's Political Philosophy**
  https://www.theglobeandmail.com/opinion/pierre
  -trudeaus-political-thoughts/
- **Maclean's: Pierre Trudeau's Intellectual Influence**
  https://www.macleans.ca/politics/how-trudeaus-intellectual-foundation-shaped-canada/
- **The New York Times: Trudeau's Political Ideology**
  https://www.nytimes.com/2017/11/06/opinion/pi
  erre-trudeau-ideas.html

6. Trudeau's Close Relationship with Fidel Castro and His Public Admiration for Communist Regimes

- **The Guardian: Trudeau and Castro's Friendship**
  https://www.theguardian.com/world/2016/nov/27/fidel-castro-pierre-trudeau-canada
- **BBC News: Fidel Castro and Trudeau's Relationship**
  https://www.bbc.com/news/world-latin-america-38114953
- **The Canadian Encyclopedia: Trudeau's Foreign Policy with Communist Nations**
  https://www.thecanadianencyclopedia.ca/en/article/pierre-elliott-trudeau-foreign-policy

7. The Ethical Implications of Supporting a Dictatorship While Promoting Himself as a Defender of Freedom

- **The Globe and Mail: Trudeau's Ethics and Foreign Policy**
  https://www.theglobeandmail.com/opinion/pierre-trudeaus-legacy-in-question-over-ethics/
- **BBC News: Trudeau's Public Image and Dictatorships**
  https://www.bbc.com/news/world-us-canada-43356320
- **The Guardian: Trudeau and Ethical Contradictions**
  https://www.theguardian.com/world/2016/nov/28/fidel-castro-pierre-trudeau-canada

8. How Pierre's NEP Devastated the Canadian Economy, Especially in Western Canada, to Centralize Power in Ottawa

- **CBC Archives: The National Energy Program**
  https://www.cbc.ca/archives/entry/the-national-energy-program-nep
- **Maclean's: NEP's Economic Impact in Western Canada**
  https://www.macleans.ca/news/canada/when-pierre-trudeau-turned-western-canada-into-the-enemy/
- **The Canadian Encyclopedia: NEP and Its Legacy**
  https://www.thecanadianencyclopedia.ca/en/article/national-energy-program

9. Allegations of Cronyism and Favoritism Toward Eastern Canadian Interests

- **The Globe and Mail: NEP and Favoritism**
  https://www.theglobeandmail.com/news/national/petro-canada-and-the-politics-of-oil/article21029732/
- **National Post: NEP and Eastern Favoritism Allegations**
  https://nationalpost.com/news/canada/how-the-national-energy-program-fueled-regional-divide
- **Maclean's: Trudeau's Eastern Canadian Favoritism**
  https://www.macleans.ca/politics/trudeau-government-and-favoritism/

10. Trudeau's Handling of the FLQ Crisis and His Decision to Invoke the War Measures Act, Suspending Civil Liberties Across Canada

- **The Canadian Encyclopedia: The October Crisis**

https://www.thecanadianencyclopedia.ca/en/articl
e/october-crisis
- **CTV News: The War Measures Act and
  Trudeau**
  https://www.ctvnews.ca/politics/how-trudeau-
  used-the-war-measures-act-during-the-1970-
  october-crisis-1.5120071
- **Global News: Trudeau and the October Crisis**
  https://globalnews.ca/news/6081757/october-
  crisis-just-watch-me-pierre-trudeau-1970/

**11. The Use of Heavy-Handed Government Tactics to
Silence Political Dissent Under the Guise of National
Security**
- **The Canadian Civil Liberties Association: The
  War Measures Act**
  https://ccla.org
- **The Globe and Mail: The October Crisis and
  Civil Liberties**
  https://www.theglobeandmail.com/opinion/war-
  measures-act-legacy-in-quebec/article32201971/
- **Maclean's: The October Crisis and Its Impact**
  https://www.macleans.ca/news/canada/october-
  crisis-and-its-impact-on-civil-liberties/

**12. Justin's Rapid Political Ascent, Fueled by the
Trudeau Name Rather Than Merit or Competency**
- **The Guardian: Justin Trudeau's Rise to
  Power**
  https://www.theguardian.com/world/2015/sep/21/
  justin-trudeau-canada-liberal-party-prime-
  minister

- **CBC News: Justin Trudeau's Early Career**
  https://www.cbc.ca/news/politics/justin-trudeau-liberal-leadership-1.1397166
- **BBC News: The Trudeau Dynasty**
  https://www.bbc.com/news/world-us-canada-34600582

13. Media Manipulation and the Creation of a Celebrity-Style Leader with Little Substance

- **Maclean's: The Branding of Justin Trudeau**
  https://www.macleans.ca/politics/ottawa/the-branding-of-justin-trudeau/
- **BBC News: Trudeau's Celebrity-Style Leadership**
  https://www.bbc.com/news/world-us-canada-43398557
- **National Post: Image vs Substance in Trudeau's Leadership**
  https://nationalpost.com/news/politics/justin-trudeau-image-vs-substance

14. Details of the SNC-Lavalin Affair, Where Justin Attempted to Interfere in a Criminal Prosecution to Benefit a Quebec-Based Corporation

- **The Globe and Mail: SNC-Lavalin Charges Explained**
  https://www.theglobeandmail.com/canada/article-snc-lavalin-corruption-charges/
- **CBC News: SNC-Lavalin's Legal Troubles**
  https://www.cbc.ca/news/business/snc-lavalin-scandal-timeline-1.5017697
- **National Post: What Is a Deferred Prosecution Agreement?**

https://nationalpost.com/news/politics/what-is-a-deferred-prosecution-agreement

15. Connections Between the Trudeau Government and Corporate Elites

- **The Globe and Mail: Trudeau Government and Corporate Elites**
  https://www.theglobeandmail.com/canada/article-trudeaus-connections-to-corporate-elites/
- **National Post: Corporate Influence in the Trudeau Government**
  https://nationalpost.com/news/politics/corporate-elites-and-influence-trudeau
- **The Guardian: Trudeau's Pipeline Politics**
  https://www.theguardian.com/environment/2019/jun/18/justin-trudeau-trans-mountain-pipeline-expansion-environmentalists

16. Examining the WE Charity Controversy, Where the Trudeau Family Financially Benefited from a Government Contract Awarded Without Proper Due Process

- **CBC News: WE Charity Scandal**
  https://www.cbc.ca/news/politics/we-charity-scandal-explainer-1.5662595
- **The Globe and Mail: Canada Student Service Grant and WE Charity**
  https://www.theglobeandmail.com/canada/article-we-charity-scandal-timeline-how-we-got-here/
- **CBC News: Trudeau Family's Ties to WE Charity**
  https://www.cbc.ca/news/politics/we-charity-trudeau-family-1.5643587

- **National Post: WE Charity Payments to Trudeau's Family**
  https://nationalpost.com/news/politics/justin-trudeaus-family-paid-by-we-charity
- **The Globe and Mail: Ethics Commissioner Investigation into WE Charity**
  https://www.theglobeandmail.com/politics/article-ethics-commissioner-to-investigate-trudeau-over-we-charity-controversy/
- **CBC News: Trudeau's Testimony on WE Charity**
  https://www.cbc.ca/news/politics/we-charity-trudeau-testimony-1.5672001

17. Patterns of Favoritism and Conflicts of Interest Within Justin Trudeau's Government

- **The Globe and Mail: SNC-Lavalin Affair Explained**
  https://www.theglobeandmail.com/canada/article-snc-lavalin-scandal-explained/
- **National Post: Ethics Commissioner Report on SNC-Lavalin**
  https://nationalpost.com/news/politics/ethics-commissioner-rules-trudeau-violated-conflict-of-interest-act-in-snc-lavalin-affair
- **CBC News: WE Charity Scandal Timeline**
  https://www.cbc.ca/news/politics/we-charity-scandal-explainer-1.5662595
- **The Globe and Mail: WE Charity Controversy**
  https://www.theglobeandmail.com/canada/article-we-charity-scandal-timeline-how-we-got-here/

- **CBC News: Julie Payette Resignation**
  https://www.cbc.ca/news/politics/julie-payette-resignation-governor-general-1.5883436
- **National Post: Trudeau Government's Questionable Appointments**
  https://nationalpost.com/news/politics/criticism-of-political-appointments-in-the-trudeau-government
- **The Narwhal: Lobbying by the Canadian Association of Petroleum Producers**
  https://thenarwhal.ca/capp-lobbying-government-record-2019/
- **The Globe and Mail: COVID-19 Relief for Corporations**
  https://www.theglobeandmail.com/business/article-trudeaus-government-bails-out-canadas-oil-industry-during-covid-19/

18. Justin Trudeau's Funding of Mainstream Media Outlets: Ensuring Favorable Coverage and Suppression of Dissent

- **The Globe and Mail: Government Media Bailout Package**
  https://www.theglobeandmail.com/politics/article-federal-government-pledges-600m-to-support-canadian-journalism/
- **CBC News: Media Bailout Controversy**
  https://www.cbc.ca/news/politics/trudeau-media-bailout-criticism-1.4915487
- **National Post: Media Coverage of Trudeau Scandals**
  https://nationalpost.com/opinion/media-bailout-trudeau-government

- **The Globe and Mail: Ethics of Media Bailout**
  https://www.theglobeandmail.com/opinion/article
  -ethical-questions-raised-by-media-bailout-fund/
- **Rebel News: Independent Media on Trudeau Government**
  https://www.rebelnews.com/
- **The Post Millennial: Government Influence on Mainstream Media**
  https://thepostmillennial.com/trudeau-media-funding
- **Maclean's: Trust in Canadian Media Declines**
  https://www.macleans.ca/news/canada/trust-in-media-declining-in-canada-report/
- **The Globe and Mail: Media Trust Erosion**
  https://www.theglobeandmail.com/opinion/article
  -canadians-trust-in-the-news-media-is-declining/
- **The Post Millennial: Media Bias Under Trudeau Government**
  https://thepostmillennial.com/trudeau-media-bailout-coverage

Here are the remaining URLs based on all the previously discussed topics:

19. Details of the SNC-Lavalin Affair, Where Justin Attempted to Interfere in a Criminal Prosecution to Benefit a Quebec-Based Corporation

- **The Globe and Mail: SNC-Lavalin Charges Explained**
  https://www.theglobeandmail.com/canada/article
  -snc-lavalin-corruption-charges/
- **CBC News: SNC-Lavalin's Legal Troubles**
  https://www.cbc.ca/news/business/snc-lavalin-scandal-timeline-1.5017697

- **National Post: What Is a Deferred Prosecution Agreement?**
  https://nationalpost.com/news/politics/what-is-a-deferred-prosecution-agreement
- **CBC News: SNC-Lavalin Scandal and Trudeau's Role**
  https://www.cbc.ca/news/politics/snc-lavalin-scandal-explained-1.5024071
- **The Globe and Mail: Jody Wilson-Raybould's Testimony**
  https://www.theglobeandmail.com/politics/article-jody-wilson-rayboulds-full-testimony-before-the-justice-committee/
- **Maclean's: Wilson-Raybould's Resignation**
  https://www.macleans.ca/news/canada/the-snc-lavalin-affair-how-the-controversy-unfolded/
- **National Post: Ethics Commissioner Report on SNC-Lavalin**
  https://nationalpost.com/news/politics/ethics-commissioner-rules-trudeau-violated-conflict-of-interest-act-in-snc-lavalin-affair
- **CBC News: Political Fallout from SNC-Lavalin**
  https://www.cbc.ca/news/politics/snc-lavalin-scandal-explained-1.5024071

20. Connections Between the Trudeau Government and Corporate Elites

- **The Globe and Mail: Trudeau Government and Corporate Elites**
  https://www.theglobeandmail.com/canada/article-trudeaus-connections-to-corporate-elites/

- **National Post: Corporate Influence in the Trudeau Government**
  https://nationalpost.com/news/politics/corporate-elites-and-influence-trudeau
- **The Guardian: Trudeau's Pipeline Politics**
  https://www.theguardian.com/environment/2019/jun/18/justin-trudeau-trans-mountain-pipeline-expansion-environmentalists
- **The Narwhal: Lobbying by the Canadian Association of Petroleum Producers**
  https://thenarwhal.ca/capp-lobbying-government-record-2019/
- **The Globe and Mail: COVID-19 Relief for Corporations**
  https://www.theglobeandmail.com/business/article-trudeaus-government-bails-out-canadas-oil-industry-during-covid-19/
- **National Observer: Lobbying and Scandals in the Trudeau Government**
  https://www.nationalobserver.com/2020/11/02/news/lobbying-and-scandals-justin-trudeau

3. Patterns of Favoritism and Conflicts of Interest Within Justin Trudeau's Government

- **The Globe and Mail: SNC-Lavalin Affair Explained**
  https://www.theglobeandmail.com/canada/article-snc-lavalin-scandal-explained/
- **National Post: Ethics Commissioner Report on SNC-Lavalin**
  https://nationalpost.com/news/politics/ethics-commissioner-rules-trudeau-violated-conflict-of-interest-act-in-snc-lavalin-affair

- **CBC News: WE Charity Scandal Timeline**
  https://www.cbc.ca/news/politics/we-charity-scandal-explainer-1.5662595
- **The Globe and Mail: WE Charity Controversy**
  https://www.theglobeandmail.com/canada/article-we-charity-scandal-timeline-how-we-got-here/
- **CBC News: Julie Payette Resignation**
  https://www.cbc.ca/news/politics/julie-payette-resignation-governor-general-1.5883436
- **National Post: Trudeau Government's Questionable Appointments**
  https://nationalpost.com/news/politics/criticism-of-political-appointments-in-the-trudeau-government
- **The Narwhal: Lobbying by the Canadian Association of Petroleum Producers**
  https://thenarwhal.ca/capp-lobbying-government-record-2019/
- **The Globe and Mail: COVID-19 Relief for Corporations**
  https://www.theglobeandmail.com/business/article-trudeaus-government-bails-out-canadas-oil-industry-during-covid-19/
- **The Globe and Mail: Trudeau Government and Ethical Scandals**
  https://www.theglobeandmail.com/canada/article-trudeaus-ethical-scandals/
- **Maclean's: Patterns of Favoritism in Trudeau's Government**
  https://www.macleans.ca/politics/ottawa/patterns-of-favoritism-trudeau-government-scandals/

4. Justin Trudeau's Funding of Mainstream Media Outlets: Ensuring Favorable Coverage and Suppression of Dissent

- **The Globe and Mail: Government Media Bailout Package**
  https://www.theglobeandmail.com/politics/article-federal-government-pledges-600m-to-support-canadian-journalism/
- **CBC News: Media Bailout Controversy**
  https://www.cbc.ca/news/politics/trudeau-media-bailout-criticism-1.4915487
- **National Post: Media Coverage of Trudeau Scandals**
  https://nationalpost.com/opinion/media-bailout-trudeau-government
- **The Globe and Mail: Ethics of Media Bailout**
  https://www.theglobeandmail.com/opinion/article-ethical-questions-raised-by-media-bailout-fund/
- **Rebel News: Independent Media on Trudeau Government**
  https://www.rebelnews.com/
- **The Post Millennial: Government Influence on Mainstream Media**
  https://thepostmillennial.com/trudeau-media-funding
- **Maclean's: Trust in Canadian Media Declines**
  https://www.macleans.ca/news/canada/trust-in-media-declining-in-canada-report/
- **The Globe and Mail: Media Trust Erosion**
  https://www.theglobeandmail.com/opinion/article-canadians-trust-in-the-news-media-is-declining/

- **The Post Millennial: Media Bias Under Trudeau Government**
  https://thepostmillennial.com/trudeau-media-bailout-coverage
- **CBC News: The Impact of the Media Bailout**
  https://www.cbc
- • **The Globe and Mail: Government Media Bailout Package**
  https://www.theglobeandmail.com/politics/article-federal-government-pledges-600m-to-support-canadian-journalism/
- • **National Post: Media Coverage of Trudeau Scandals**
  https://nationalpost.com/opinion/media-bailout-trudeau-government
- • **Rebel News: Trudeau Government's Suppression of Dissent**
  https://www.rebelnews.com/
- • **The Post Millennial: Independent Media in Canada**
  https://thepostmillennial.com/
- • **The Guardian: Canada's Bill C-10 Sparks Free Speech Concerns**
  https://www.theguardian.com/world/2021/may/10/canada-bill-c10-free-speech-debate
- • **The Globe and Mail: Bill C-36 and Online Speech**
  https://www.theglobeandmail.com/politics/article-trudeau-government-pushes-forward-with-bill-to-curb-online-hate-speech/
- • **The Toronto Star: CBC's Role in Canadian Politics**

https://www.thestar.com/news/canada/2021/07/1
2/canadian-broadcaster-funded-by-taxpayers-
cbc.html
- • **National Post: CBC and Government Bias**
https://nationalpost.com/news/politics/trudeau-
and-bias-in-canadian-public-broadcasting
- • **The Globe and Mail: Erosion of Press
Freedom in Canada**
https://www.theglobeandmail.com/opinion/article
-canada-eroding-press-freedom/
- • **National Post: Trudeau's Threat to Free
Speech and Media Independence**
https://nationalpost.com/opinion/opinion-free-
press-threat-trudeau
- • **WEF: The Great Reset Initiative**
https://www.weforum.org/great-reset
- • **The Guardian: Klaus Schwab's Great Reset**
https://www.theguardian.com/business/2020/jun/
03/world-economic-forum-calls-for-great-reset-
of-capitalism
- • **UN: Global Compact for Migration**
https://www.un.org/en/ga/search/view_doc.asp?s
ymbol=A/RES/73/195
- • **UNFCCC: Paris Agreement**
https://unfccc.int/process-and-meetings/the-paris-
agreement/the-paris-agreement
- • **CTV News: Immigration Targets**
https://www.ctvnews.ca/politics/canada-
announces-plan-to-welcome-1-2m-immigrants-
in-next-three-years-1.5163850
- • **National Post: Canada's Carbon Tax and
Economic Consequences**

https://nationalpost.com/opinion/canadian-federal-carbon-tax-hurting-economy

- • **Maclean's: Justin Trudeau and Post-National Canada**
  https://www.macleans.ca/news/canada/what-does-trudeau-mean-by-post-national/
- • **CBC News: Trudeau's Global Vision for Canada**
  https://www.cbc.ca/news/politics/justin-trudeau-post-national-state-1.3450448
- • **The Canadian Encyclopedia: National Energy Program**
  https://www.thecanadianencyclopedia.ca/en/article/national-energy-program
- • **CBC Archives: National Energy Program and Western Resentment**
  https://www.cbc.ca/archives/entry/the-national-energy-program-nep
- • **National Post: Trudeau's Carbon Tax and Western Alienation**
  https://nationalpost.com/opinion/federal-carbon-tax-alienates-western-canada
- • **The Guardian: Pipeline Cancellations and Western Canada**
  https://www.theguardian.com/environment/2018/dec/10/canada-oil-pipelines-trudeau-keystone-xl-trans-mountain
- • **CBC News: Coastal GasLink Pipeline Protests**
  https://www.cbc.ca/news/politics/gaslink-pipeline-blockades-1.5459386

- • Global News: Economic Impact of Resource Blockades
  https://globalnews.ca/news/6595716/pipeline-protests-economic-impact/
- • Maclean's: Wexit and Western Alienation
  https://www.macleans.ca/news/canada/wexit-the-movement-that-wont-quit/
- • CBC News: Trudeau's Challenges in Western Canada
  https://www.cbc.ca/news/politics/trudeau-western-canada-alienation-1.5439781
- The Canadian Encyclopedia: National Energy Program
  https://www.thecanadianencyclopedia.ca/en/article/national-energy-program
- CBC Archives: The National Energy Program
  https://www.cbc.ca/archives/entry/the-national-energy-program-nep
- CTV News: Trudeau's Carbon Tax
  https://www.ctvnews.ca/politics/federal-carbon-tax-in-canada-how-it-works-and-who-it-affects-1.4355400
- The Guardian: Pipeline Cancellations and Western Canada
  https://www.theguardian.com/environment/2018/dec/10/canada-oil-pipelines-trudeau-keystone-xl-trans-mountain
- Maclean's: Wexit and Western Alienation
  https://www.macleans.ca/news/canada/wexit-the-movement-that-wont-quit/

- **Global News: Wexit and Western Separation**
  https://globalnews.ca/news/6354134/wexit-separatist-party-elections-canada/
- **CBC News: Trudeau's Challenges in Western Canada**
  https://www.cbc.ca/news/politics/trudeau-western-canada-alienation-1.5439781
- **National Post: The Rise of Alberta Separatism**
  https://nationalpost.com/news/politics/alberta-separatism-and-the-rise-of-western-alienation
- **• The Canadian Encyclopedia: Multiculturalism**
  https://www.thecanadianencyclopedia.ca/en/article/multiculturalism
- **• CBC Archives: Pierre Trudeau and Multiculturalism**
  https://www.cbc.ca/archives/entry/1971-trudeau-announces-multiculturalism-policy
- **• The New York Times: Justin Trudeau's Post-National Vision**
  https://www.nytimes.com/2015/12/12/world/americas/canada-justin-trudeau.html
- **• CBC News: Trudeau's Immigration Policy**
  https://www.cbc.ca/news/politics/justin-trudeau-immigration-plan-1.5167848
- **• The Guardian: Trudeau's Post-National Canada**
  https://www.theguardian.com/world/2017/sep/12/trudeau-canada-national-identity-multiculturalism
- **• The Globe and Mail: Canada's Relationship with the Monarchy**

https://www.theglobeandmail.com/opinion/article-canadians-relationship-with-the-monarchy/

- • **Maclean's: What Does Trudeau Mean by Post-National?**
  https://www.macleans.ca/politics/what-does-trudeau-mean-by-post-national/

- • **CBC News: Bill C-16 and Gender Identity**
  https://www.cbc.ca/news/canada/gender-identity-rights-bill-c-16-passes-senate-1.4162595

- • **Global News: Indigenous Reconciliation under Trudeau**
  https://globalnews.ca/news/7812868/indigenous-rights-trudeau-legacy/

- • **The Globe and Mail: The Challenge of Canadian Identity**
  https://www.theglobeandmail.com/opinion/what-is-canadas-national-identity/article36849652/

- • **The Canadian Encyclopedia: Multiculturalism**
  https://www.thecanadianencyclopedia.ca/en/article/multiculturalism

- • **The Conversation: The Effects of Multiculturalism on National Identity**
  https://theconversation.com/canadas-approach-to-multiculturalism-needs-a-rethink-93136

- • **Maclean's: Western Alienation and Trudeau's Policies**
  https://www.macleans.ca/news/canada/wexit-the-movement-that-wont-quit/

- • **The Canadian Encyclopedia: Quebec Sovereignty Movement**

https://www.thecanadianencyclopedia.ca/en/articl
e/quebec-sovereignty-movement

- • **CBC News: Political Polarization in Canada**
  https://www.cbc.ca/news/politics/justin-trudeau-
  election-polarization-1.6161777
- • **Global News: Urban-Rural Divide in
  Canadian Politics**
  https://globalnews.ca/news/7439227/election-
  analysis-urban-rural-divide/
- • **Maclean's: What Does Trudeau Mean by
  Post-National?**
  https://www.macleans.ca/politics/what-does-
  trudeau-mean-by-post-national/
- • **The Globe and Mail: Canada's Evolving
  National Identity**
  https://www.theglobeandmail.com/opinion/canad
  a-and-its-changing-national-
  identity/article36849652
- • **The Canadian Encyclopedia: Pierre
  Trudeau and China**
  https://www.thecanadianencyclopedia.ca/en/articl
  e/pierre-elliott-trudeau
- • **CBC Archives: Trudeau and China**
  https://www.cbc.ca/archives/entry/pierre-trudeau-
  goes-to-china
- • **National Post: Cash-for-Access Scandal**
  https://nationalpost.com/news/politics/cash-for-
  access-scandal
- • **The Globe and Mail: Chinese Donations to
  the Trudeau Foundation**
  https://www.theglobeandmail.com/politics/article

-trudeau-foundation-1m-donation-linked-to-cash-for-access-fundraising/

- • **The Guardian: Justin Trudeau's Trade Relations with China**
  https://www.theguardian.com/world/2016/sep/02/canada-china-free-trade-justin-trudeau

- • **BBC News: The Arrest of Meng Wanzhou and China's Retaliation**
  https://www.bbc.com/news/world-us-canada-50676070

- • **The Globe and Mail: Chinese Interference in Canadian Elections**
  https://www.theglobeandmail.com/politics/article-canadian-elections-china-influence/

- • **National Post: Chinese Interference and the Trudeau Government**
  https://nationalpost.com/news/politics/china-canada-interference-election

- • **National Post: Trudeau and Corruption Scandals**
  https://nationalpost.com/opinion/opinion-trudeau-government-scandal

- • **CBC News: Restoring Public Trust in Government**
  https://www.cbc.ca/news/politics/public-trust-in-government-canada-1.4923281

- • **Financial Post: Economic Consequences of Trudeau's Carbon Tax**
  https://financialpost.com/opinion/trudeaus-carbon-tax-the-economic-impact

- • **The Globe and Mail: Canada's Energy Future**

https://www.theglobeandmail.com/business/articl
e-canadas-energy-sector-future/

- • **The Globe and Mail: Western Alienation and Trudeau's Legacy**
  https://www.theglobeandmail.com/politics/article
  -western-alienation-in-canada/
- • **Maclean's: The Challenge of Canadian National Unity**
  https://www.macleans.ca/news/canada/canadian-
  national-unity-challenges/
- **The Globe and Mail: Is Trudeau's Political Career Nearing an End?**
  https://www.theglobeandmail.com/politics/
- **National Post: Justin Trudeau's Declining Popularity**
  https://nationalpost.com/news/canada/justin-
  trudeau-approval-ratings
- **The Canadian Encyclopedia: Multiculturalism and Its Future in Canada**
  https://www.thecanadianencyclopedia.ca/en/articl
  e/multiculturalism
- **CBC News: Justin Trudeau and Canada's Identity**
  https://www.cbc.ca/news/canada/justin-trudeau-
  multiculturalism-legacy
- **The Guardian: Canada's Carbon Tax and Climate Policy**
  https://www.theguardian.com/environment/2021/
  mar/31/canada-carbon-tax-trudeau
- **Global News: LGBTQ+ Rights and Trudeau's Social Legacy**

https://globalnews.ca/news/justin-trudeau-lgbtq-rights-canada/

- **Maclean's: Western Alienation and Canada's Regional Divide**
https://www.macleans.ca/news/canada/wexit-the-movement-that-wont-quit/

- **The Globe and Mail: Quebec's Place in Canadian Federalism**
https://www.theglobeandmail.com/news/national/quebec-federalism/

- **National Post: The Future of Conservative Leadership in Canada**
https://nationalpost.com/news/politics/conservative-party-canadian-future

- **Maclean's: The Legacy of Justin Trudeau**
https://www.macleans.ca/politics/justin-trudeaus-legacy/

- **• The Globe and Mail: Canada's Decentralization**
https://www.theglobeandmail.com/politics/

- **• Maclean's: Addressing Western Alienation**
https://www.macleans.ca/news/canada/wexit-the-movement-that-wont-quit/

- **• The Canadian Encyclopedia: Quebec Sovereignty**
https://www.thecanadianencyclopedia.ca/en/article/quebec-sovereignty-movement

- **• Financial Post: Balancing Canada's Economy and Environment**
https://financialpost.com/opinion/justin-trudeau-economic-impact-carbon-tax

- • **The Globe and Mail: Corporate Influence in Canada**
  https://www.theglobeandmail.com/politics/
- • **National Post: Rebuilding Trust in Canadian Politics**
  https://nationalpost.com/news/politics/canadian-political-corruption-ethics
- • **Maclean's: Redefining Canadian Identity Post-Trudeau**
  https://www.macleans.ca/politics/what-does-trudeau-mean-by-post-national/
- • **The Globe and Mail: Canada's Decentralization**
  https://www.theglobeandmail.com/politics/
- • **CBC News: Strengthening Accountability in Canadian Politics**
  https://www.cbc.ca/news/politics
- • **Financial Post: Tax Reform and Economic Growth**
  https://financialpost.com/economy
- • **CBC News: Energy Sector and Canada's Economic Future**
  https://www.cbc.ca/news/business
- • **The Guardian: Free Speech and Government Censorship in Canada**
  https://www.theguardian.com/world/canada
- • **National Post: Civil Liberties and Government Overreach**
  https://nationalpost.com/news/politics/civil-liberties-canada

- • **The Globe and Mail: Reforms for a Stronger Canada**
  https://www.theglobeandmail.com/
- • **CBC News: Path Forward for Canadian Civil Liberties**
  https://www.cbc.ca/news/politics/canadian-civil-liberties

---

www.ingramcontent.com/pod-product-compliance
Lightning Source LLC
Chambersburg PA
CBHW062127020426
42335CB00013B/1122